T0067318

IMMEDIATE MESSAGES SENT FROM HEAVEN

Immediate Messages Sent from Heaven

Greg Belter

IMMEDIATE MESSAGES SENT FROM HEAVEN

Copyright © 2014 Greg Belter.

All rights reserved. No part of this book may be used or reproduced by any means, graphic, electronic, or mechanical, including photocopying, recording, taping or by any information storage retrieval system without the written permission of the publisher except in the case of brief quotations embodied in critical articles and reviews.

iUniverse books may be ordered through booksellers or by contacting:

iUniverse LLC
1663 Liberty Drive
Bloomington, IN 47403
www.iuniverse.com
1-800-Authors (1-800-288-4677)

Because of the dynamic nature of the Internet, any web addresses or links contained in this book may have changed since publication and may no longer be valid. The views expressed in this work are solely those of the author and do not necessarily reflect the views of the publisher, and the publisher hereby disclaims any responsibility for them.

Any people depicted in stock imagery provided by Thinkstock are models, and such images are being used for illustrative purposes only. Certain stock imagery © Thinkstock.

ISBN: 978-1-4917-4185-6 (sc)
ISBN: 978-1-4917-4186-3 (e)

Printed in the United States of America.

iUniverse rev. date: 07/29/2014

With great respect for the Lord and the Virgin Mary and Father God, it is truly such a great honor being able to receive prophetic and spiritual messages from the heavens. Your undying devotion to your people and the interpreter will not go unnoticed.

FOREWORD

It has been brought to the interpreter's attention to be convincing with "spiritual messaging." Our dedicated Masters inside of the Holy Spirit will be sending continual messages down to earth, penetrating through air space to communicate special visions which are very colorful, and even wording which will appear for all of us. The gift of discernment is a wonderful thing, as long as the results are truthful and well respected in the eyes of the Lord with His Father God and the Virgin Mary in full acknowledgment with messaging to us.

Many small white clouds are touched off with some darkness coming from the spiritual world. Suddenly on the edge of a blacker cloud a smidgen of light that whitens appears combined with very beautiful eternal light resembling the sky. The Holy Spirit interjects saying, "We are proud of you." This type of communication using visible dark wording from the Lord is very strange to some, but the miracles He will perform are of many and often like this. The white light is slowly spreading to where an angel's wings have formed opening. At first the angel's tummy was plump, although it went into the appearance of a glowing golden heart. The angel is small and very cute. A streak of gold light glides across the angel's wings. Once stopping they became very saturated, and the right wing even lifted somewhat higher than the left. Where is the halo? The angel's face just gleamed brightly in a golden hue. Funny when looking up for an answer that occurred, and all at once the crested halo shined so bright in gold, we would believe that the light upon the angel's face was a blessing. The spirit of our Lord relates, "Girl." Our visiting angel is a youthful girl. Her face has changed to more of a soft vanilla shade of light.

The Lord says, "Visitors are welcome in your home." Audiences need to know they are being told the truth with spiritual matters. After a series of delicate motions inside of the Holy Spirit on the Lord's part a silver shield bearing a nice white cross has embellished the front, whereas it was presented in the kingdom. A marble size white ball of light rests upon each end of the cross. Now two hands hold on firmly over the top edge. A white and gold handle on a sword is sparkly, and there is a wonderful pearl necklace looped over it hanging down behind the shield. You may be wondering how the interpreter saw the sword's blade. Before the Lord placed the pearls where they were at, He was demonstrating from His side of life the full length of the sword.

Four white windows become visible. Each has a windowsill that has a strip of golden light. The sacred cross of our dear Lord Jesus glows in each one. A tall white door with a soft glowing gold knob fits into the heavenly scenery as well. "Welcome to My home," the Lord sends us. A bright red rose is grouped with a white and yellow flower of the same kind. They stand beautiful. In the middle sits a small white basket, where paper unrolls downward from over the outer edge. The image of Jesus inside the white light of His is so impressive. A long pencil suspended in air points to His right ear. Now the Lord is cupping His hand around His ear, because He so desires inside of His heart to have everyone send Him a message. This you won't believe at all. "If you would like to write it down, I will read your concerns," spelled out wording inside of the Holy Spirit returns. The Lord would like you to look upward and to Him right now so that you can see what He is doing with the three flowers. They bounce around in the Lord's hands close up to nose. He's really enjoying the fragrance of them. Hard telling if this is funny or not. A hand is being held over someone's right eye. Try that to better look-see inside of the Holy Spirit right now, and perhaps you will see, not only the vibrant yellow, red and white flowers, but you may be treated to an unexpected visual visitation from the Lord too.

When the Holy Spirit sweeps across the physical plane or inside of the pathway they have created for you new things are bound to enlighten us. We will still be able to accept these experiences down the line somewhere, after we have gone to heaven, whereas our Lord and Almighty God will likely be teaching us more about these things. They'll be divulging such wonderful spiritual activity that has and will come our way again.

A black doctor's bag has opened up with holy white light starting to come out from the top. A stethoscope is being worn with Jesus placing it into His ear to hear with. He says, "It caused a small chuckle here." Now the item was placed over His heart where a beautifully glowing gold cross rests beneath it. Of course He is doing that. He says, "Tell them I suggest watching their food intake." Isn't that the truth? White sugar is pouring from a large bag into a huge pile. If you saw the pile you'd think the same. It seems the Lord is forewarning us to be aware of serious heart issues that may occur from overdoing it with eating too many sugary items. Now a filled brown paper bag which is tightly sealed is lined up with the depleted sack. If we could only keep away from sugar. "It causes trouble with some," the Holy Spirit included.

The Eiffel Tower appeared in a misty white light. Thankfully nothing terrible was seen thereafter. But what did come about were visible words. They read: Very Proud People. Naturally the other side of life was referring to the French. They needed acknowledgment from the light. Several couples act out a little skit from the other side. Even inside of a mellow yellow or light shade of gold, they were seen cuddling closely. The Holy Spirit reacts, "People should be affectionate." While pondering such closeness, especially in the open public, no one should judge what God has intended in life for people.

A very small girl with shoulder length brown hair that is quite wavy sits before the Lord's throne. The Lord's knees and white robe are very visible. The girl is an absolute angel. "It pleases the Lord to share openly about both of us," Jesus says. The series of words show too. Two tall white candles sit behind the girl, but not too far away. The tinted yellow light from the flames radiate outwardly now, creating many different pathways around the Lord and her. The paths are very level. At the end of one was a small ivory and very golden glittering angel of the light. A fairly decent distance away but noticeable. Between each ray of light a baby blue puffed up cloud appears. Larger wings are coming to life around those areas with one particular angel's head drooping down low. Still within the angelical baby blue wings, arched back, and looking so holy, the angel is saturated by golden light that seems to be almost runny. Perhaps this is the way our Lord feels about His cup that runs over within the light, which continues to pour out upon everything and everyone.

Pale pink is significant light up and way beyond. Sent here it not only conveys that a brighter light shines through it, but more angel wings form, largely, that belonging to a golden haired lady with very thick curls across her forehead. Her crown is silver, and even though it doesn't stand tall, she is prominent. She says, "Thank you." She would like us to keep moving along. From her and not the interpreter's main thought coming to mind at first. She sends a red heart out to everyone. She says, "They'll think that is true enough." Her white halo is large in size. That alone puts her in the spotlight. Small amounts of white creases of light beneath her nose moves about as she breathes in clean air. She said, "The air is very fresh." She is a very good consultant when sought after for doing so. Double checking is very valuable. She said, "I'm not a queen, although a very loving soul." Her thick eyelids are a mild shade of pink, while her sparkling eyes of blue have been revealed upon them opening. As she turns herself about inside of the Holy Spirit she shows off a mesmerizing golden white glittery star at the center of her crown. Who are we to judge who receives a crown to wear in heaven? The Lord could be misinterpreted as being sarcastic with this next comment, but that's not what He is implying through voiced words which just came in through the spiritual vibrations. "The Lord and I will judge who wears a crown," spoken of inside of the Holy Spirit. Do you get the sneaking suspicion that God just spoke to you? The interpreter has that feeling and knows that it is very much of a plus sign.

The word "howdy" appeared inside of the mildest sunlight in the heavens. After approving such a message, again and again, it would be right to finish up with this peculiar interpretation. A ranch hand sitting on a brown horse with darker hair to the long neck. The horse has arched his neck for a better view to be taken of white light on the ground, where it has covered only the horse's mouth and nose now. The cowboy with the tan hat on says, "Boy were you ever confused at first. Don't worry I am friendly," he says, using real words in the light. He was referring to the interpreter, and He was right. Behind the horses's ears golden light glows beautifully warming his senses too. "He is my friend in heaven. I know it sounds peculiar to hear from me and you will need to explain why I am here," said outright. The age of "sixty" presents itself. The cowboy is holding his hand upward and over his heart. "My heart was bad," he throws in. He cares for the horse the same way as before, therefore it is his. That's so true, and by the way he's doing an extraordinary job brushing his horse. Funny thing was the cowboy brushing the horse in the opposite direction from the tail end all of the way across him, stopping and going again. Maybe just to get our attention at first for relating his actions.

"Open your mind more," the Holy Spirit advises wisely. When people meet in heaven for conversation and pleasurable walks together they come posthaste. You may be advised to visit with family members by spiritual guidance from the Lord. "You'll hear the voice of the Lord speaking often," Jesus is saying. A gold dash of light grants a holy feeling when shown. Not merely a figment of the imagination, it comes from God or the Lord, and perhaps from both at the same time. "When you arrive in heaven your thinking will improve to where you'll have a genius mind," coming from above us now.

The other side feels the feeling is mutual for the Lord's people with many of His angels visiting, that they are very Godly when filled with spiritual images of themselves created so heavenly like, whereas they haven't been limited for just a few to be seeing them.

"Don't worry about the enemies from your past," Jesus sent in a message. You know why that just came about? The interpreter was willing to drum up subject matter, and when doing so the Lord created words from solid gold to appear before him. He reads our minds. How many of us really want to be hobnobbing with people in heaven who we had a hard time getting along with in life? A mini trip to hell would be more fun that. The Lord appeared and He has a grin on His face. His lips were pressing together. "I won't make you do anything that is harmful to you," He is saying. A thank you was given back to Him in a short but meaningful prayer. He says, "You won't have any trouble getting along with people in heaven."

Leave your troubles behind, the Holy Spirit moves unwanted darkness away with the useful touch from an angel, using ivory wings which are now in a restful position. Pretty unique considering the angel seems to be proud, by the presence of expanding white light helping along with the elimination. Life is still very much outlasting with the other side. Someone whom we will "find out who" just stuck their tongue out, and was even pressing their fingers against the inside of one's mouth to make a funny face with. Before that occurred the certain party did happen to smile. Inside of a serene and mild orange light is where this person is. "We are trying to cheer you up some," the spirit messages wording. Have you ever felt like and looked as if you have lost your last sucker? As an adult the child of our own self does still exist. Sometimes we need to be just a little happier, and with the other side intervening like they have the interpreter will accept that they live it up to a far greater extent with merrymaking than thought to be.

Why does a clown appear? Wearing a black polka dotted clown suit with a matching pointed hat is a man or a woman. That person is tall enough to at least determine that it isn't a child. The clown is still present, coming from the hereafter. "Don't you know who I am?" the clown asked. How would the interpreter know unless he was already introduced? "I do care for your well being, friend," the friendly spirit says. A sudden interruption by the Holy Spirit brings in warmth from inside of the spirit by covering the clown with a golden light, except for the black spots in attire. The clown is a woman with brown eyes, full cheeks, and a white bow, which looks quite large hanging from her neck on down. She is spinning a tan-white ball around on her finger. There is vivid light coming from the ball, going into three directions as it spun around fast. The letter "Y" appeared from the light which the ball's colors generated. Then a black letter "e" came out of the blue. All in all, she said, "Ye." Interesting! "Our ways make you think in depth," she said now. A gold rocket and a smaller white one pointing upward was illustrated by the friendly helper as to be telling us more about being "rocketed" into spiritual life. The lady clown is moving away from the earthly visitation, and as she does, golden eternal light drizzles out from the inside of her right eye. Small white wings carry her away now. Until some other day when we meet again. She was likely the person who had her fingers sticking inside of her mouth joking about earlier. Without the rest of her face showing, besides her mouth at first, smiling, and the funny gesturing, it was hard to tell who that was in the beginning of the show.

Informed about an oversize white tulip flower without a stem is where people climb inside of to go for a ride. "Go ahead and tell them," the spirit advises. The interpreter asked them, "Is this true?" A small boy and girl in shiny gold light are leaning over the flowers petals with their hands held up to the side of their heads, nonchalantly. Seeming so common for them. Where have we been? "They shrink too," the little boy laughs about. A golden trim that's glistening so brightly round the flower is within an angle, dropping and raising back near the flower's edges. "Don't stop now," they say. They do float through the air with ease. They are now passing through blue clouds which are rare, but known of from earlier exploration of the heavens.

White clouds were passed by too. "We needed to stop for refreshments," the boy says, as the interpreter laughed. While looking for their destiny to be revealed, they had already stopped in front of an unusual refreshment stand, where a golden haired lady with shoulder length curls leans to the side as to be listening attentively to the youngsters. The words, "thank you" appeared twice above each child in gold letters. Therefore they thanked the lady who served them at their stop. Funny how each child had a white straw which was made, not from a material source, but from the light above. The kids have blonde hair. You were to be told. "Let's go higher to see some people," the boy insists while the girl is watching and listening closely.

"Try to capture the meaning of the messages," the Holy Spirit announces. A group of jagged, almost tan color rocks, have splashing water upon them at a place resembling a vast ocean. Until this happened something else did, proving that the ocean front was not on earth, but it now came in a vision from the Lord over on His side of the spirit. A tall amount of white light edges out from the inside of a huge tunnel of eternal presence. Soon the rocks are covered by the light. "We have several oceans. The reason you were shown was to prove a point," the Holy spirit continued speaking. People are peacefully enjoying themselves at the many oceans and various beaches available in heaven. There is much enthusiasm with the children playing and running about.

While a boy was rasing a very large beach ball into the air while playing in the sand, a baby blue angel appeared mostly solid, whereas we may think of it as "plain," the features in this angel were precious. A holy angel in heaven at the beach? That's a new one, but very sensible, whether we are in heaven or not, at least one should be behind or beside us all the way.

The wide and soft yellow candle has a black and white wick, while three dark blue stripes of light at a forty-five degree angle are not brightly shining, but they have become an unusual idea in the Lord's mind for a presentation. Up one and up two. Sounds funny doesn't it? The Lord's hands are beneath the candle rasing it upward, and after the second direct movement, the Lord's face was covered by a very pretty smooth golden light. The candle's softer glow from that alone, and not from the wick, had brought solace to our Lord. Something He enjoys more and more.

"You will bow down before Me for peace of mind," the Holy Spirit is remindful today of His grand desires. Three mint green shapes come through, stretched a little like taffy. The form which came about was a triangle. "Unity inside of the Holy Spirit," was wording seen in bold black print, thereof. A lovely and very delicate blue-green shaded leaf appears on an angle. "Whoever wants to see the leaf shall," came from the Lord. A young male figure around thirty, sitting in a chair, is looking up into the light where the leaf reappeared. Besides the Lord's go-ahead, the word, "ok" was shown too. Fat brown trees are coming through from the spirit world, but there was only one visible green leaf hanging down from each of them. Where was the fruit? Finally, one by one the Lord finished His creation with a red apple, then a yellow apple, an orange was given its place upon a branch, and then a hanging pear.

Four pairs of dark rimmed glasses now appear with only white light for lenses. He must be suggesting again, for all of His people to begin seeing inside of the light for given pleasure. Once you raise your head up a little you could see what He is talking about. It feels as though you are witnessing the beginning of time, how God began making His own creations, which He made absolute sure of that they would be shared with the world. "That was funny what you were thinking," the Lord relates about the interpreter believing from the sight of them that the trees were fat. A quick turnaround to say the least.

All of this unusual movement in the spirit, what does it mean? Since white light exists around the vision of dark visuals of a solid black manger, and a thin angel holding that up from underneath it with only one wing, it is all good. A very nice glowing pink vibration sets the spiritual tone, as a light which spreads onwardly and far in width. The angel's face is very white, except for the glowing fine features coming and a golden nose. The sparkles of gold upon the crested halo made a small trail of light down upon the angel's nose. Beautiful white light has now covered the baby Jesus like a smooth blanket. A spiking golden light shines above Him as He lay in the manger. Stretchy gold stars twinkle all around Him now. The Virgin Mary picked up Jesus and comforts Him near Her bosom. She came in all white light, and even a greater whiteness appeared around Her face and head. "You are better off carrying the message. My Son is faithful to His Father," Mary related to us.

"We are working on new ideas for you," the spirit just related. Ivory walls appear on each side of a long staircase filled with silver stairs. While the top of the walls swirl with embellishments of many glistering rocks, the inner staircase has started to glow with a heavenly white light brightening the first four steps. At the very top two ivory pedestals stand tall with a clear bubble ball of light upon them. Now a gold cross in mid-air is between the pedestals. Father God and the Lord have come up with a good idea. A small ball of white light has moved on to two steps, but it seemed there was floating or bouncing taking place, because of the identical ball, fading halfway, and then appearing more whole two steps away and then finally near the bottom. So the Lord has brought us from down below, to bringing our attention up to the top of His creation, and then we return to where we have started from with light upon the staircase.

While realizing the Lord's hands are being held out, fingertips facing the interpreter, Jesus has two white balls of glowing light in His hands. What do we see now? The Lord's hands were pressed against His eyes with white light spreading out from them. He either created two white angel wings from that source of light, which appeared behind Him, otherwise the angel was there with Him all along. He wants you to know He has always thought of Himself as special to His people. Jesus says, "Tell them I am trying to heal them through prayer. Don't stop believing."

The Lord is counseling a heavenly woman with shoulder length straight blonde hair, on how to make music sound more interesting when played inside of an orchestra. A nice gold light covers everyone, including isles of seated performers. Two flute players have stood up, and even though their music can not be heard from earth, their hands hold their instruments up and cross in front of themselves. Meanwhile the Lord and His daughter next to Him are likely waiting on the interpreter to look up to them for the continuation of this interpretation. "Good thinking," the Lord related in a message. The woman with brown eyes is happy about Jesus pointing out on the white stand of golden sheet music before them that everything was now clear and ready to be instructed. She had one of those rounded music instruments up to her lips, where she is beginning to blow into it for finding the right pitch. That's unusual to lead an orchestra this way. Back in music class teachers often used them for singing. The do, re, mi, fa, so, la, ti, do scales. There is soft yellow light above everyone seated now. It was less golden. The Lord assigns angels to be near the people, although there were only four of them visible, also inside of the soft light was their natural wing color of "soft yellow." However their halos were white with a silver cross embellishing the front. However the holy angels are they have their eyes closed now. Dark eyelashes suggest they are people too. The woman by the Lord's side is leaning an elbow upon part of the stand in front of her, to where her sleeve is glowing in white. She isn't upset over not paying more mind to herself and the Lord, she is interested in how the message went. "I have dimples that are noticeable," she says. And this is true, they are very grooved, small, and very cute. People in heaven, how very nice.

People would be surprised to learn that they have relatives playing instruments in orchestras. "You'll know the various instruments easily," Jesus says. Our Lord talks a lot now with reference to the life in the hereafter. A shiny black piano sits somewhat away from a white one. "Duets are formed here," is a message. A young girl and boy are really carrying on with their voices lifting in a cheerful song from which they have learned. They are sitting on the bench in front of the white piano. The top of the piano is propped up high, arching. Baby blue rays of light are beaming from in front of the piano, four thick ones to be exact. Funny but a small white angel with a black face has a white halo with a robe which curls up at the ends on the bottom. Soft blue light just blanketed the piano keys, and the girl over on the boy's right, leaned around him some to view the other side of life better.

An orange curved horn was shown and immediately the message was fully understood. Grab the bull by the horn or horns. Inside of the light that was their method of doing things, wrong color for the horn or not. "We know what you were thinking," the Holy Spirit reveals in words. Yes they are that smart. And why wouldn't the Lord relate more crucial messages to people? "We try to assist whenever we can. Evildoers were warned there would be some consequences that were coming down the road for them," was related. Count your blessings. "People on the straight and narrow are to be rewarded later," came from Jesus using His voice and a string of words shown.

Here we are again with the house guests who come from heaven to entertain us. Pierre is his name and no doubt in his mind, he was from France. In heaven his black hat has a tiny white feather sticking up on top. He says, "Perfect the language of French if you have time." Apparently he used a hammer in his trade, since one stood upright in gleaming gold light. Where did he go to? It seems the people and the subject of France is important of their whereabouts, and how they behave. The Frenchman is standing at attention saluting France's national flag. He is right handed, that's a sure given. The number seven and the word "requests" appears. Ask for numbers. Think of it as a simple request. God will help the Swedes just as much as the French and anyone else involved in prayer. Perhaps the Frenchman was sent here to remind people to pray for prosperity. Remember to go with your feelings.

Thank God nothing was climbing up the far wall. The Holy Spirit's unexpected movement hit a sensitive nerve. You could be told about that spirit of a man wearing a super fluffy white beard, mustache and long hair, dressed in a shiny floor length black robe with plenty of white stars when standing here. A pearl necklace is around his neck, hanging down over his chest with a silver cross gleaming between those at the bottom. Praise the Lord and God. Hail to the Virgin Mary. "Ask in prayer who I am," the spirit said. But that request would need answering through the Lord. "Father God is very interested in your life," the Lord responds back. Wow! Now Jesus is wearing that shiny black robe with stars and a wonderful necklace, otherwise, He is God. He does hold onto a tall shepherd's cane nearly pressed to His chest over on His left side. Does God take on the Lord's image? "You often wonder how I look," was the message from Almighty God. Suddenly the crown upon His head has massive gold appeal, but what's more adorable was Jesus, or God with three babies wrapped in white blankets, finding solace inside of the Holy Spirit's arms right now. That can be Jesus, or that could be God.

The prettiest blue skies have an angel acting quickly below them. Why was it considered skies instead of a sky up in heaven? First, the angel is solid gold with ruffled wings. "We think of it as a heavenly sky," the angel answers. That's a good thing the angel's words appeared, because quite frankly, the interpreter was at a loss for words. The angel has a small but effective white pointer, pointing in several directions. White pathways lead to where spirit people stand inside of the white Christ light. People are praying in various positions having fun, while everyone have one basic thing in common, their hands are folded. A gold light by the Lord glows brightly, to where the Lord's legs in a sitting position were still white, until a second image of Him standing revealed the Lord in all golden light. But He kept both images in place, as though He took on a little out of body travel

Himself while remaining upon His throne. The image of Jesus in the soothing golden light was of Him looking at Himself on the throne, but several feet away.

How is this even possible? An angel's frosty white halo tilted forward enough to see that a girl was reading the Bible while leaning in to see the word. Moments before that the Bible was balanced upon a flat edge to the angelic girl's right wing, facing upward when laying level. She says, "Tell them I have silver wings." She is a learner of the word, and felt that someone needed to adjust their eyesight. She was a little less forward about conversing that to the interpreter to begin with. So you see these magic eyes are not always perfect. Her eyes on the other hand have gold in them. With gold light glowing within each of them, they began expanding inside into thin, stretched out crosses. She said, "Tell them they have change to their original blue color."

Why are they creating a strawberry, a peach and one blueberry? "Eat our fruit more often," the Holy spirit conveyed now. We will be healthier inside if we do. "Your problem is neglect of that area of nutrition," is a pretty precise word message seen inside of the spirit just seconds ago.

Keep on pushing forward seems to be coming through, by way of the intensity of the spirit. They have a visitor that we are going to meet shortly, bringing us some important news. Clear angel wings are whipping the air. Then after finally stopping, now just golden tips to the wings pointing upward can be seen from this side of life into theirs. Again and again, after a little bit of disbelief it is an ongoing vision of someone inside of the Holy Spirit surrounded by creative angel wings, holding onto a lighter of sorts, that which flickered once, and has finally succeeded in lighting up a pipe full of marijuana. The plant is near the smoker, but we all know very well, there is absolutely "no smoking" inside of the heavenly realm of living. Some smoke starts to rise from the pipe, very thick indeed. The spirit points to and shows outright the states of Washington and Colorado, to where we have known for some time now to have legalized marijuana. There must be a strong point needed to be made from above on this matter. The map of the United States is starting to change to a charcoal shaded color across many areas. They have illustrated within a few years many states will legalize marijuana. It was just to clue you in on what was to come down the line. We figured that would happen. Washington and Colorado were of the same dark shade to begin with. More shading indicated more followers.

Someone in a wheelchair inside of a creamy golden light has stood straight up. Marijuana has been known to release muscle spasms and intense pain quickly.

Now two new images are evident. Thrones made from golden light. Side by side they have two occupants. Jesus is smiling while turning His attention to His left, where someone with great esteem sits with a very white and silky beard that tends to come to a softer point at the smoother ending curl. His hair is of short curls, and very thick. It has considerable length on down to His shoulders. His eyelashes slowly raise to reveal beautiful brown eyes of a peaceful nature. His mustache is of thick white light. The Lord is happy. As He nudges forward a small golden cross in His left hand shows His Father. His right hand is flat and open, as if to be thanking His spiritual Father for giving unto Him eternal life, while God has been very thought worthy of Him dying on the cross. Jesus is very much in appreciation of God's own gift of life unto all.

Beautiful arching angel's wings on the floor in front of the interpreter are glowing beautifully. They were pink, white and blue. Check down below and between your feet to check to see if a small white angel has arching wings. Not as strange as you might think, though. Maybe in front of your feet then, and perhaps two small angels. Imagine folded white napkins if you can't quite see anything in the form of an angelic presence. You'll see angels. Concentrate around your feet. Sparkling golden light shines. That which you'd love to drench your face with it's so pretty.

A white angel with gold wings is being funny. One wing is richly embellished with golden swirls and of a more rewarding design, while the other wing is plain. The very enhanced wing spreads out causing much wonderment of its beautification. And, all of sudden it flipped outward, spraying the other wing, until finally all of the drizzling golden light which began from the top decorated the entire wing.

A soft blue and white light comes at least for now. Three sparkles of gold lead to a smooth and very wide swath of a golden pathway. There inside of the enchanted heavens awaits a sensitive lady carrying a tan basket, which was also wrapped around her right arm. She takes care of it carefully with her left hand upon the top of the looped basket. Her hair is very curly and brown, shoulder length that it is so full and bouncy. Some people have all the luck with a full head of growing hair. A white spot of light is glowing near the center of her forehead so much that it has now covered her entire face. "You will complete your mission on earth later in life," she says, using wording. For one and for all in this case. People need more of their wisdom. That was her thought process too, it wasn't just picked out of the air. She has a small yellow ribbon in her hair on the right side. She has the interpreter fidgeting over here wondering about what she was carrying inside of her basket.

Does she have kittens too? A golden angel's wings pop up outside of the basket. Then a golden halo that glistens. We know the angels are beautiful, but this one keeps changing the wings around, holding the tip of each one up to "her" ears, first to the left side and then on to the right earlobe. A cute girly angel somehow and someway is small enough to fit inside of a normal size carrying basket. It must be nice to be toted around. With wings like that, she could go anywhere, especially down to earth for a spiritual visitation. The angel seems to be saying, "Hear ye, worship the Lord." Glowing light of gold appears beneath them, too, and as it rises, they disappeared leaving a bright gold star to appear in the Lord's company. Yes He did come through from the spirit world, and He is bending low, almost to be bouncing while doing similar knee-bending exercises as we would. "That would help you at times," He says in the spirit.

This truly is better than going out for the evening for other activities. That will have to wait. "Peace on the other side is abundant," Jesus speaks to us using visible words again. There is another interesting aspect of spiritual travel on the other side many would like to hear about, concerning what we would experience if in heaven. An out of body experience has prompted this message to come forth. In heaven it felt really fulfilling being guided by a lady who wasn't seen, but was heard talking. We shall see people in heaven, but this is what took place which was considered to be an immediate message. The inner soul began going through a winding tunnel of pink light, that which was formed as such a very long and seemingly never ending course of travel. Small walls on each side were of pink eternal color. They kept on going leading upward to a wonderful place when the out of body experience ended in one direction. Glowing white light was everywhere in sight and so were magnificent looking stores where you could look at anything you ever dreamed of.

The Lord says, "You won't need any money for clothes, but you can shop for just about anything your heart desires." He just said that. It was a good thing He did, because the interpreter knew he'd have a hard time finishing with the interpretation.

The first thing that comes to mind. Soft white bunny ears belonging to one showing up in the light came in view, with a brown rabbit next to the animal. There's a small pink and yellow ribbon attached to a new basket with a huge white egg inside. White light shines upon the oval egg, more upward due to the light's ability to glow and shine everywhere expected and unexpected. A little boy comes in with brown hair, and he stood a little over four feet tall, even though he is levitating himself in mid-air and inside of the Holy Spirit. With a small egg, more regular and normal in our view, the boy now places an egg up in the spirit up in front of each eye. With a very full smile and bright teeth it's more obvious that he is here to entertain. His right eye has been fully revealed after lowering the egg to rest inside of his hand. His eyes are brown, at least one is. Here is the reason why the thought had occurred of possible mixed eye color. They have been known to do funny things in the spirit to entertain us. And while the boy moved about and more with slightly bended knees now, he has revealed that his left eye isn't brown after all. For the moment it is a misty white color with a sizable silver star inside of it in replacement of the boy's pupil and other eye color. He says to someone inside of pure white light, "Boy is he ever funny." The boy is very telepathic when sending messages.

Apparently the young entertainer is celebrating life with many Indians as the spiritual interpreter is really getting an eyeful with the many Indians, both young and old coming in through the light nearby the boy. The youngster is juggling more than just the two eggs he came here with. What a change. He is juggling many eggs so fast that a hamster on a wheel would have a hard time keeping up with him. The perpetual movement is really that interesting to look at. The boy stands comfortably in his soft white robe, where he created a "v" in shape of three eggs attached to himself on a big necklace. Much easier on the eyes as you might have thought otherwise. He nonchalantly extends his hand and brings it back showing off how he can hold onto a couple of oval eggs between his fingers. Three blue flames of light appear above the young entertainer in a bending arch, but with a peak of sorts too. A golden star brightens at the top of the canopy of eternal greatness for the boy in the showplace of heaven. Unbelievable but true. He says, "I'm preparing a surprise for someone." A tan spatula worked its way around inside of some type of honeypot of a mix. The tip of his right index finger reached his mouth, and one heck of a double take was taken from unbelief from here on our side. He is really tasting a mix while preparing something eatable. Now only one egg remains on the boy's chest, and it appears a thin strand of leather runs itself through both sides of the shell. Or is that eggshell of light formation? It is no wonder that nothing is running out all over the boy's robe. He must have taken away the other two eggs when twisting them around in his hand, while ready to make his tasty mix for his friends. He had to help with differentiating whether there was just one friend or two friends who would be receiving an unexpected treat from him. The word "friends" in black lettering appeared. It is still very mind-blowing as to what is going on up there above the grand blue sky of ours. What an amazing golden cake he is holding up high to examine. It has thick icing which swirls all around the cake. He says, "A special occasion is coming for us." Every day is special in heaven. "It is thoughtful that you would share my thoughts with everyone," was his message too. The Holy Spirit wishes that we close with him there.

Gold and white leaves casually drift by in the spirit, but they also are backed with smooth white light. A larger gold leaf in the center of them points down. We will get to who is busily arranging other plant life forms in a second. Hands are moving about high above the spread arrangement down below. Good Lord! What else would you say when He comes through the light holding a potted lily plant? Jesus has wide ivory wings that have sprinkled gold dust upon the fringe of them, especially around the top curving wings. "The plants are for a reason," Jesus explains. He also said, "Share your thoughts." He feels the interpreter is a "lucky person" to see into the light. But, we should feel very confident that there are others with the same gift. Needless to say, everyone will be seeing inside the Holy Spirit one day. Maybe even tomorrow.

"Cherish every minute you have been given in life," the Lord articulates in spiritual wording which became visible to translate. The tense state of the mind comes from extra expansion, to where it is good to grow. They may be growing pains, but good ones. Black twisted candles with small white flames, and twisted white candles with black flames fill the scenery.

The Lord feels you might dislike being told about something just seen. But what He really means is how it would be told, rather to "suggest" that people listening to this message might try listening to reason, and not feel you are being ordered to participate in the forthcoming. Look up and visualize two colors of "blue" for further enlightenment. The Lord shows eighty to ninety percent of the people joining in on the experiment will see this spiritual vision from Him.

You know what's very surprising? The interpreter here has been enduring pain on the right side of the chest for over a month, and while sitting here thinking more deeply about the intense situation, a vision of a lung appeared in the center of an upright beam of thick white light. Then the Lord spoke, using visible words, relating, "Penetrate my white light inside of your mind and body." So you will have to excuse the interpreter for a minute, while a "quickie" mediation begins. It wasn't at all bad resting within white light. The Lord was quick to help out with the meditative state in more ways than just one. He illustrated the back of the head, visible brain matter inside of the skull with a white ball of light at the back of the neck. Visible white light was traveling inside of the brain, and with such a great vision from the Lord it was easily shown on how to begin. No pain for the moment. If it comes back that same meditation will apply.

Very thin but powerfully peaceful rays of light glow an array of color. The color of orange, vanilla and pure white and a yellow ray was extraordinary. Not so much as the color but the way the rays of light just filtered into the air so peacefully. Simply an unusual order of light. "Step into the light," Jesus recommends. The health issues come back. "Project your health becoming more stable," the light brought forth that easy message.

There's mention of the Lord's children praying to Him all hours of the day and night. Is there nightfall in heaven? A family of three, includes the parents for a boy standing with their backs to the starlit night. They're dressed in the finest soft white robes to be found in the heavens. Soft sunlight shines through the night's sky to where the boy is enjoying the touch of it upon his opened hands that are cupped together. "The sun will change without notice," it was told with the boy communicating now. But what does he mean, that it could become more of a brilliant heaven filled such unimaginable delight? Asked to the boy, through prayer inside of the spirit world, "What do you mean?" "The light will change your life immediately," he says while looking down slightly over his right shoulder to earth, while smiling.

Wondering what God is doing? What He would want you to hear all of a sudden, like it isn't anyone's business but your own? Okay, He will be asked for your pleasure. "Let me say that I am happy you have contacted me," said using words which appear. There is a lot more coming. He resembles Jesus, although all covered in white light upon His face which is visible to the interpreter. He would like everybody to know that the two soft balls of white light in each hand, and the one centered above His head is where the power of life comes from. He says, "You are learning bit by bit." He stands next to Jesus, but only their heads are visible, encircled by golden halos. Think of them as your good friends. A gold cross is above them, and in front are many bunches of soft pink flowers that are to their liking.

When wondering about if the Lord would like certain people to see the two of them together right now in a vision, with them suggesting how to help you see, a message came through the light. "Some people are bound to see us come through," was the communiqué. Look for the gold. The halos stand out brilliantly, as they most certainly do too. "Picture us in front of yourself," said. Three smooth white triangles appear, which would mean they'd like you to find them from looking at an angle. "Suggest that there is white light between us," was messaging coming through words. This is not a fool's game. It is very kind of Jesus and God standing next to us through this very extended period of our lifetime. "You have guides but many people do not understand them," Jesus speaks. He has a point there. It all sounded fuddy-duddy to the interpreter many moons ago, but they have proven from all the way up inside of heaven that they're willing and able to help us during sleeping hours, and most importantly while awake.

There is a lady friend in the light who was known from this side many years ago as the neighborhood beautician. She is visiting and wanted something said about herself. Being reluctant to speak of her in the mild golden light, just wouldn't do overall since she was able to show wording to express why she was here, and also present there in the light as a spiritual soul. "I am fixing hair," she says. Now there is a blonde with a very full head of hair sitting in front of her. "I had an unexpected death due to cancer," the beautician relates, which is true. There is more from her. "When you come to heaven the Lord will pray with you to find peace within," she said through the eternal light which surrounds them. How about cutting hair? Let's see what she says about that. "It helps to keep it neat," she said with speed. She felt that her comments were real and understood within a very spiritual nature. "The perfection astounds me, and you will know what it's like when you arrive home," she relates as twinkling gold stars gleam above her and the friend. She also shows a yellow and white long stem flower to help us feel better.

"You'll feel the enchantment of heaven often. I have a castle for you to enjoy," the Lord relates. Wouldn't it be nice if we had our very own castle? It will likely feel that way because of the Lord's great kindness and wealth. "We chose to share our home with you," Jesus continues relating words in the light. Something interesting just occurred. To the interpreter it resembles an old-fashioned door made from dark, country wood, with many smooth lines across the entryway, shining gold hinges with an arched window baring a cross in the center of it, which was to lead inside of the people's very own mansion. How could that be so, and is the interpreter really seeing what he just said he saw? After taking a second look into the light waiting for the Lord's approval, the door appeared once again with the same name across the grain of the wood. It read: Our Mansion. You will live like royalty. "You shouldn't overstate it, but people will have a choice if they want something the size of a castle to live in forever," very close or exact to what the Lord just said.

The Holy Spirit feels best that using intense concentration into the light would be okay too. Two hooking wings and a streak of a vibrant green light penetrating this vibration came from a known source in heaven. Five blue lights glow across the background. That was to aggrandize what the other side was feeling. Don't think that it was evil, you are learning things. Now orange glowing entirely around the black wings glorify them more. The wings fold back, while leaving smaller amounts of the orange light centering more of the wings. The angelic body turned ivory with a face, hands and an open Bible. Never have you ever seen such a beautiful ivory Bible and angel. We should be satisfied with this spiritual personification. The wings were ivory now.

Expect a change in topic to come. Two people are sword fighting on the other side of life. They are masked, dressed in white, and it's hard telling if they are male, female or both, without seeing their faces. That will come though. The person on the right has bent down to see someone or something coming close from behind. The mask lifted with that person and sure enough a pretty woman with brown eyes appears. She is getting bigger in the spirit. She says, "You should know we love each other here." Swords of existing eternal light are soft to the touch. A cool black belt with a white cross embedded glows with silver glitter which rules over their noble game of swordsmanship. Who was fencing with her? Sure enough the other person's mask was removed too. A man with a very pearly white light upon him as well, is readily awaiting any questions that we have for them. He is using words to communicate with, that's how the interpreter knows from sight alone. Just a simple reminder, a question will be presented to them.

They presented yellow butterflies and a picture of a human stomach. They think there are butterflies in someone's stomach, and probably true too. The interpreter's lips purse from trying to think of a good question. Asking in prayer helps. "Why is God so big?" was asked. The man put his mask on again, while holding his cupped hand up close to his right ear. He had heard the prayer request, through the Lord, but also directed to him and his gal friend present. "He is grand and knows all," the man says, when using large golden letters. But, that's impossible for God to be where He is in the spirit, creating Himself before all of us and everything in total existence. "It would seem so. He is a loving Father to everyone," the lovely blonde sends in a fun-loving letter of sorts. The swords have been laid down where silver glitter bursts grandly.

Even if we have seen one beautiful spiritual vision from God, He'll want to be casual with bringing back what's important inside of our memory to validate. A small golden chalice is held between the Lord's hand near His knees. If He isn't interested in what He is about to give unto us then we must be blind and not able to see Him bringing forth new inventiveness. And if there are people who can not see what He is doing right this minute, then perhaps this transcription can be read out loud for them. Jesus brings the royal chalice upward close to His chest holding it near and dear to Him. The soft golden hue from the chalice covered His face. People on their knees are accepting the Lord's gift of light, that which is poured from his drinking cup. They're covered in light too. A woman wearing her hair in a bun stands up and softly moves around to the Lord's left side, where she has a string of sparkling golden stars draped upon both of her hands, which she eventually wraps around the Lord's golden crown. Our Lord's crown is now a masterpiece. She is Asian, bowing halfway over in respect to the Lord with hands pressed firmly as to be in prayer giving thanks to Him. She wears a red flower.

Indigo light fills the heavens. It is so, a man tips his derby as a gentleman would. But, after that image a Tommy-gun appears. "Don't worry about what you say," was given in an instant message. A man inside of the white light has a crinkled nose showing he strongly disagreed with people at times. He turns standing much taller, without that crinkle in his nose now. He has changed, and he's peacefully holding a white petaled flower inside of his hands. That's much better than a machine gun. The word "Dutch" could be seen, but that could mean anything, right? Whoever he was, the man's life has taken a three hundred and sixty degree turn in the right direction. "I forgave him," Jesus says. Thou shall not kill may mean exactly that, but our Lord and Almighty God have forgiven everyone already. They love everybody and everyone.

We can read other material besides the Bible in heaven. The knowledge will be extensive for all. By sight you will learn even more. Spools of thread and someone with yarn in her hands is perceivable. A lady is present. "They will come to find out that you are right about me," she believes. She is holding up a caramel color sweater, seemingly the size that would fit a very young person. She said to the interpreter through spiritual communication, "It took about as long to create as it did for you to think about me making it." She was pretty fast at that. She is full of wisdom and politeness today. "I like you too," she commented.

Why the sweaters in heaven? She made another one with black swirls all over the whiter clothing. "You don't need to worry," she explained to the interpreter who was adrift. Or perhaps the feeling of being "out there" was all on account of astral traveling into the spirit world. Her soft movements suggest peace and quiet.

An angel glides and slides back to our side. Is the angel moon walking or what? The golden crest is also creamy yellow on one side.

A half and half halo. Why so many angels? Who cares this one's face is so beautiful so humanlike too. Wow, what a clear complexion. Her robe's white too, but the golden cross on her chest is massive in size. From her feet up to the tip of her chin. Her robe is wider than anyone's ever seen by the interpreter. Maybe there are fat peeps in heaven. Time to look up and stop transcribing for a few seconds. She keeps referring to the number two. No she isn't wearing creamy orange rabbit ears, they are angelic wings above her shoulders. "There are two wings for each of us here," she explains. They are fun to use that's for sure. Two pounds heavy and easy to fly with within the spiritual realm of wonderment. "The angels do listen to you," she mention while holding her right hand to her ear.

We should see ours first. "If you look around you'll see many angels," she communicated just now. She has a small illustration laying flat, but when the word "guide" appeared next to the document it was obvious that God has planned out your life. And angels can even guide us every time we seek them out. If your angel is a man, or a woman with angelical wings don't fret if you've never seen them before, when you do see the angels inside of the spirit, just go with the flow, they'll show you the appropriate imagery. Try seeking the kingdom of God first, your angels are trying to breakthrough for your convenience.

"Let them hear my plan for their lives," Jesus informs the interpreter. Soft ivory hearts have beautiful creamy orange flowers filling in behind them everywhere you look. The Lord has a big red heart, but only half of it can be seen. No He takes hold of an ivory heart which has enlarged itself in front of our Lord. His fingers hold the bottom edge ever so lightly. The ivory heart began to crack. "Broken hearts can be mended," Jesus relates in His words coming through the light more visibly. For those of us who really understand where He is coming from it shouldn't get us down, especially because of Jesus being here now. Your interpreter is having a hard time from keeping the tears from flowing from seeing Jesus. Be ever so grateful.

There's a new technique for meditation being shown right now. Three cones of white light penetrate the back of a male helper's head in the spirit world. He is actually sitting down on a cloudy white chair.

It isn't a real cloud, the chair's dimension is solid and very soft to be sitting on. First the right side of his face is glowing all white from the whirling cone of light. Then the man's forehead, nose, eyes, mouth and chin turn a very smooth color of white from the second cone behind his head. The light penetrated through him while coming out through his face. The third whirling white light filled in the rest of his face. It should be used simultaneously though. "Be a guide if you want to be," they just said. It's strange, but this was what Jesus just said, "Expect a miracle if you are uncertain of the light." You know what? He also said, "You are special that's why I come to you through the heavens to help." White light is shooting out from the helper's fingertips now. He placed his hands, baby fingers together close to his chin, which could almost make us think he had lit birthday candles in front of him. At the tips the white light was slightly brighter, an extension of the glowing rays. Hard saying why he is covering his face now, but for sure, the decorative glowing fingers are touching in a very special way.

There is a blue pointy crown with a gold cross at the top, and especially attached firmly for the Lord's greatness to be respected more. Jesus is wearing that crown, and His lips just turned gold. Another double-take. Those beautiful furry white ends to the Lord's sleeves to His robe are interesting. The Lord's arms and His business what He wears. Just because the interpreter says they are furry white it doesn't mean He took an animal's life for them. He is the light, therefore, He was given this robe from His Father whom He is fond of. "The cuffs are not fur," He relates here. Look for the gold sparkle and you may see Him inside of the light wearing His very fine white robe with fringe.

Small very gold feathery angels appear before you upon the floor if you would only watch them come to life, as they already have with the interpreter. The Lord highlights them with their own little sparkle of gold. Their halos aglow with baby blue color, but change after a few seconds. Watch them change from blue to white now. Their wings are blue and a shade of mint green. They're turning gold too. Do think of the interpreter and the angels as teachers of the light. They have moved up to the Lord's thrown where they form a perfect circle around each of His sandaled feet. The angel's wings are now half white and vanilla.

The Lord wanted that vision for everyone to know of. "You shouldn't worry about the language spoken," Jesus wishes the best. Baby blue candles with their white wicks beaming a blissful light are soothing for the Lord to view. The Lord's hands come into view. Resting upon His throne golden light inches outward from beneath His palms. He says, "You know of my love." And there's more. "Forgive me for waiting on your blessing it's coming down the road," our Lord sends to us in a personal message which we have yearned for some time now.

Big teeth are being examined inside the light. We will think that dentistry has been taught to us while in heaven. We will enjoy learning about things going on inside of hospital rooms beneath us as well. "You will pass over in a blink of an eye," was an instant message, and we'll be very healthy in heaven. Teachers will also assist us around in the light. The levels at where we should be learning will depend on the Lord's understanding of where we'll be located within His realm.

"There were many valleys in your life, but you were guided by the light to help you succeed," Jesus sends in another believable message. Think of the spirit world as a fun place where gentlemen in black and white tuxedos bow and tip their tall hats to you. One gentleman in a white tux with a long tail has a gold cross in the middle of his chest. On a tux it looks rather nice. The inside of his hat is quite white, that only being revealed for the moment, as the other gent's tall black hat was shown in its entirety. That man on the right insists others learn of him carrying a small bouquet of white flowers which he is truly very fond of their fragrance. It's hard telling how many times people in the light have been seen sipping tea, and these two gentleman in their fancy tux are no exception. They are raising and lowering cups and saucers. "We think that you know by wishing for the desires of the heart that God and the Lord will satisfy your needs," the long winded gents tells us, via, spiritual foreknowledge. A silver teapot is pouring tea out into an ivory cup. One of those ghostly visions. You said it. It kind of reminds you of the special effects used on television, but this is the real McCoy with levity. These words came: Please use the tray. A shiny silver tray tipped forward and on the flat surface a mild golden light is glowing with the name, "Lord Jesus" printed upon the lower and upper section.

Now we have it right. The saying, "Believe in miracles" appears twice, glowing in soft blue and gold lettering. The words would remind you of glowing bulbs inside of a storefront window. So the Lord, Almighty God and the Virgin Mary still strongly believe in great things happening in our lives. "The sick deserve better," Jesus says from inside of the light. There are two irons one would use for ironing clothing brought to the foreground of a spiritual vision. Perhaps these pressing issues we have can be ironed out after all. The Lord is looking at one of His lambs before His feet. "All of my animals are loved by me," He relates.

A flash of not so blinding white light was accompanied by many pale blue flowers, which have such remarkable beauty in the heavens. Glad to be there and here. Still within the heavens of many spiritual gifts and surprises. A well-known trumpet playing man inside of the Holy Spirit of golden light is entertaining many people standing up in a massive crowd, but for some reason the listeners are below him at a different level, as to be watching him play up on stage in a dignified manner. His trumpet was lowered way down low and then lifted to send sound out to the audience who await "great sounds" to be heard in heaven.

"Peace is quite the theme here," a mystery guest said, by using bold black lettering while amongst the crowd. The man or woman has at least three large patterns of black color in a few squarish shapes covering this person's face, almost in all of its entirety. The focus is still upon this special person. The candle coming from their side is blue and white, or half and half. There's a white wick which has gold-leaf like features. At first the offering from the mystery person looked like something else. The entire candle turned gold. Nice and beautiful. Softly the candle blends in with our air. That candle when turning all gold appeared more real on our side than from when it was blue and white. Don't tell God that, but it's probably because of Him using much holy power to initiate the newness. The Holy Spirit says, "There is much abundance in our light in heaven."

They have one golden step and a white step. Let's hope that everything comes out well with their denotation given now. Being led up the two stairs from the spirit's action, the Lord becomes slightly hesitant when halting spiritual activity for the interpreter to identify with Him and the insight given from above. Now the interpreter felt that there was some sort of drop off coming and that turned out to be right on the money. But, down below was a huge valley filled with green trees which looked like genuine felt. The trees are at eye-level for the moment. We need to picture ourselves in heaven with the guidance from our Master's light. Your visions will accompany the belief in your holy Father and Lord Jesus straightening the path out for you. Twinkling gold stars fill the area with light. Three children in mild golden light are waving. It seemed they were picking fruits from the trees, but after seeing that their hands were empty in the air, zooming in on them clarified what was up.

Then a small train was boarded again with children taking off for a ride. The front car was still a train, but they made it into a small fire engine for the lad. No, wait a minute, that's true and false, because his ride where he steers in front turned into a locomotive, one hundred percent right. That kid and his magic. The car behind his remained in the shape of a small elephant with a small dark-haired girl sitting in place with soft lips and content in her face. They are telling your interpreter that the boy has dark hair. He was covered in some gold light is why there was more assistance given. What he did was unbelievable. His fire hat is baby blue with a black emblem on the front. There appears to be a number "51" upon the front of his helmet. Why? He does have our utmost attention for now. What was funny about how he expressed himself to the interpreter and anyone else caring to believe in him was, he brought his hands together to speak through them. If you take your own hands and press the two index fingers together with your thumbs, you've noticed the shape of a spade. Such as with playing cards. He pressed his mouth against his hands, and believe it or not, wording appeared in the spirit. He said, "Look at you." The interpreter thought that was funny. There is a small girl with brown hair in the last amusement car behind the girl in the middle.

Why did the name Molly just appear? "Because of the passenger riding is why," was an immediate message back, which surprised even the interpreter.

There is meaning in the spiritual messages received. The Lord says, "Don't doubt your abilities." The ocean's tide gently comes into shore where there is plenty of sand. It is very nice seeing that. The Lord knows exactly when to bring more peace about. Huge hands cupped together are out almost dipping into the ocean, facing us now. "My Son is also giving unto you of the sea," words were relayed to earth in the spirit. You know that was God talking then. The interpreter really liked that God became very direct with us. The power of God enlightens you too. Hands hold a gleaming gold bar-cross inside of them reaching the top edges of God's hands, and upon the watery ocean still very much in view.

"I wept for my Son like you were wondering about," Mary interjects during silent meditation. Heaven will be quite easy for us after understanding Mary, Jesus and God's messages. They will continue guiding us closely. Someone said, "You'll like sports here." A youngster was seen wearing a football helmet and pads. Kind of hard to fathom after receiving the holiest spiritual message about the Lord and how Mary personally feels about Him.

Your soul is an entity itself in heaven. "Think of yourself as becoming a super-human being in the light," received in a message. You will glide a little quicker up in heaven when you begin bending your knees with arms extended. The image shown is of a person doing exactly just that, close to the image of sleepwalking almost. Your eyes will glisten brightly with the spirit around you. We will still feel the same affection for people on earth, simultaneously as we are with others from the eternal side of life. "Your feature will be lightweight which you are aware of from out of body experiences," was our message.

A couple of personal white ruffle angels sit inside the foreground of heaven, and inside of the background a gushing water fountain with grey hanging leaves and grapes are a first, at least for this enthusiast. The Lord's hands are now touching the very first grape at the very bottom. Moreover His hands have somehow managed to blend in with the leaves and grapes of the design, to where they have become golden, except for one of the grapes, that being the very first at the bottom. His hands are cupped inside. That was an awesome feat going from touching the fruit from the outer structure, to ending up with the Lord's hands inside of it.

As an example of what it feels like to be helped at times in prayer with people's requests, which all are very worthy of asking our Lord and Almighty God for, the Lord is showing many hands grasping onto the very bottom to the front of the Lord's robe. They are tugging at Him. "I feel it is necessary to hear their requests," He tells the interpreter. Jesus has His shepherd's cane in His right hand now. It is tall and pearly white according to the Lord. A baby duckling rests before the Lord's feet. You know the darling type with yellow fur. The word "Easter" appears too. They do correlate when you stop to think about Easter eggs, and colorful baskets for the kiddies. Three purple ribbons are fastened to the Lord's throne. One is much larger though, attached over on top to the right, where His throne begins before cresting so very ornately.

The Lord has either stepped away from His throne just to show us the ribbons clearly, or to give us such great satisfaction in having the honor to be fully trusted with one of His cherished items. The throne has a golden backrest, that which is decorated beautifully with small gold flowers. There are many gleaming rays of golden light behind the throne, where a tunnel of peaceful white light has led people up to be with the Lord. This is so very true because of the two people on their knees behind the throne in the background of increasing white light which has completely covered them. But there's one more person in the background who looks like he just came to heaven. The look on his face at first told his feelings outright. He asked, "Where am I?" What was rather humorous was the sudden change on his face, from slight confusion, to that very contented look. Be assured he is very happy and smiling cheerfully.

Wiggling around and finally back into the spirit world further is a bent and thin black flower vine. The flower at the top including one leaf is all black. To the left is a detached yellow tulip offered splendidly as a token of God's appreciation. Much blueness is settled in as descending yellow light borders the flowers. Those weren't two white umbrellas turned upside down after all, narrow paths led out and away from the base of broaden white light. Two expressions form next to each path. A frown and the smiling face. For sure that gigantic sparkling gold castle as tall as the tallest building ever built exists way beyond upon the pathway, which led away on the left spectrum of holy light. The Lord pulled out from the inside of a white treasure chest an oval object which was very gold and shiny. After handing it to one of His loyal followers it was wrapped around, and now can be told by sight inside of the Holy Spirit, a man's shoulder blade, to where it hangs down to his waistline. The man wearing the white angelic robe bows down before the Lord, saying, "Thank you for giving me freedom."

Let's check on the visitors who would like to come through now. The interpreter prefers to see just plain ordinary folks who have passed on to make a better life for themselves. He has no control as to who they are and to what will be spoken through channeling. No one will come in unless the Lord permits them to do so. Jesus is doing the same thing that the interpreter is, contemplating. He can be seen in white light, it looks like a light snow has fallen upon Him, but His beard is of sheen in gold. The Lord held His index finger up against His chin, as the interpreter was doing the same while thinking. We ended up being impressionists in the light together. The Lord said, "There is someone present, but you are a little less attentive." A man has a stopwatch in his right hand. Well maybe this won't be "boring." Now a few older clocks surround him. One is dark brown, and the others behind the spirit are white cuckoo clocks. He has a gigantic clock too. The top part is rounded with only a couple of black numbers on the face of it. How can we keep time like that? The man says, "You can tell when your demise is if you visualize the clock with no hands." He does sound unbelievable, but so does everything else that seems impossible. Check your Bible, right? Supposedly no one should know when God comes for us, and that goes for the Lord too. Let's see why we should look for a tell telling sign of a couple of numbers appearing on an invisible clock, which for some very odd reason should be able to tell us when we will go. The interpreter doesn't believe it either, but this timekeeper in heaven does have a valid point it seems. How about premonitions of loved one passing away.

Here's something that the clock shopkeeper is acting out inside of the spirit world. Take both of your thumbs and gently place them against the sides of your nose. All of your fingers should be straight up and together, not spread apart. That's what he was doing. He says, "Look for a round light." He meant white light though. You'll want a huge face of a clock to appear across the room where everything else is pretty much bare. Even though there is an odd shape between your hands, picture the white ball of light with hands spreading slowly. A white extending light will glow beneath the round ball. If you desire to know the age you are when you expire, two numbers may or may not appear. The interpreter still thinks it is crazy. While trying it out over here your interpreter found two dark numbers on the clock. A little more time than what was thought to be.

The man holding a small alarm clock inside of his hands like it is gold, says, "Tell them to use their own discretion." Check for the very first dark number, then see what comes up for the second. If two numbers appear at the same time keep on meditating, you only need one before the other to determine your ripe old age. Don't rush through the experiment, there might be three numbers. And where does the zero fit in at? Check the middle of the clock. If that method works well for you try different uses for daily numbers. It worked here without too much more to say about that system.

Ready or not, the Lord is still here with spiritual works. "It gives you peace inside to study us," Jesus speaks such great words. There are three black candles. The flames were not bright with light because they are dark. One yellow candle fits in between. The creativity is mostly to behold. You know that kind of artwork would sell if you painted it. The Lord's right earlobe holds a small gold cross upon it now. "You thought it was an earring. We condone such jewelry," was said. "Some people think there are ghosts in Scotland," the Holy Spirit brought out into the open. Ghosts are real and sometimes do harm. This info still comes from the light, but will be transliterated from the interpreter's perspective. They feel a kinship to homes they lived in that's why. "Good spirits come from us," the Holy Spirit communicates. "Does the Holy Spirit play tricks on people with bad spirits?" asked through prayer. "The answer to that would be no!" explained with wording in a foggy white light, whereas the words were bolder.

"Where do the evil spirits come from then?" asked now. "A different level than from ours," our Lord conveyed. "Who created the evil spirits, Lord?" the interpreter just had to ask. "You don't know, do you?" Jesus asked. Hey, Jesus is a very fun loving Lord, isn't He? Maybe more from Him. "Father God loves you," Jesus expresses openly, and that's that. It was a little unusual thinking that way, but Jesus was responsible for bringing up the topic of ghosts.

Three white doves in a v-shape are beginning to create sound in heaven. With movement from each of their beaks, gold eternal light glitters. Jesus feels it is good to use Him as an example. A swath of golden light sparkles in front of the Lord, mainly in front of His left eye. His eyes absorb the entire amount of light, to where His eyes are sparkling in gold light, but enlarging to the point where they become more rounded instead. Suddenly the Lord's eyes change, where He is now wearing dark shades. Yes indeed, He is wearing glasses. "Why the dark glasses Lord?" asked in prayer. The Lord says, "It is to remind you the blind will see again."

A person can be the scum of the earth and the Lord will still by their side. Naturally He wouldn't call people that sort of name, but the interpreter would. That could be a character defect, such harsh criticism. The interpreter isn't anywhere near much more special than other people, to be seeing in heaven and being able to receive instant messages. In fact, the interpreter has had such intense rage inside his soul, you wouldn't even believe he was the same person translating all of these true messages. "We agree with you when it comes to being critical of others," the Lord relates inside of the light. So this is about our Lord's heaven very much indeed.

When you perish you'll want to be joined with your family. That can be arranged in the spirit. A gigantic white cake has printed words on it. Maybe yours, but perhaps for your loved ones too. It reads: Welcome Home. "Served up like you expected," Jesus says, and a good side view of Him serving it close in spirit proves what has been said. Look in front of yourself, anywhere. Do you see cake? No shrink needed here, the Lord is serving cake over inside the other side of life. If we can just pass comfortably. Let's ask the Lord what He would have us believe upon our deathbed, if our life draws near its end slowly. Oh Lord is He ever nice. "Peace my friends," Jesus spoke up using yellow lettering this time, which was visible moments ago. He also says, "I'll make sure you have a home in heaven."

Jesus looks like a rock star on His throne with all white covering every inch of Him, while hordes of people below the throne are cheering Him on, waving with the women and others in shock of who He is, as many were holding their cheeks gently with open mouths. They seem to be saying, "Oh my God." No matter how the Lord comes back around to us with these people near His throne, the joy of it happening amazes.

"Don't be alarmed but God pictures you in heaven with Him," spirit talk remains steady. Pearly white lion claws decorate the highchair for an important dignitary in the light. Just a gold crown shined above this becoming seating arrangement. The Lord drew in the interpreter's attention twice to the claw chair. Holding off waiting for someone to appear sitting on the chair is becoming just too intense. You feel there is someone coming but who? Looks like a grumpy God on a side view. But what He said back was, "That's you when you are upset." His face was disturbing. Time to laugh at things a little more. Now there's a happy God with huge puffy cheeks. A smiling God in the light who changed His appearance to being bald as a baby, to making Himself into the image of the Lord, exactly down to His fine hair, beard and mustache, and now to an image of a serene Asian God, whom you won't believe is fiddling with chopsticks near a few grains white rice. A smooth pink beaming light comforts His face.

There is no need to test anyone to help encourage them to really believe now. Between the Lord and the interpreter, a message came to him not to worry about putting everyone to a test of closing your eyes to look for a blue, green, pink, gold, or for even the orange spark of eternal light to glitter, to prove these messages are true. It was thought that if you were to see any one of the beautiful sparkling colors, that would mean the interpreter has been telling the truth. Go ahead God won't get mad at you if your were to ask Him for one of the colors to shine from His own personal throne room. Therefore, the interpreter doesn't expect you to follow his own advice given, unless you really feel it is necessary on your own account.

"We're celebrating still," the Lord passes along to us joyfully. Jesus brings a smile, but it felt like a bad day because of the cold and the wind outdoors. His arms stretch out farther than expected with one soft white angel in each hand. He kids around saying, "I can reach around the world with my hands." A beautiful image of the earth appeared too. There are probably a few areas the Lord doesn't want touched in on. Just from thinking about this and that to ask Him, there was very sound advice given. "I know you have many questions to ask me. Be wise now," He explains.

Space exploration will continue in the future, perhaps more for one nation. Bright frames of fire burst from beneath two rockets as they rise into the atmosphere. A message comes in about the United States and Russia both having secrets. A message reads: Peace is what we want. Don't we all want that? There seems to be considerable spying going on from behind the scenes with five countries. As the messages keep coming even a number helped out to determine how many countries were spying on each other. They can not retaliate in any way if the messages are coming from heaven. God wouldn't want His children harmed. Why would the heavens be feeding us all of this information if it were to bring repercussions?

If you care to use more of the Christ mind inside of yourself, ask God to show you visions of people faraway from where you live. Tell God and Jesus you want to see your friend or friends at distant places by using extra sensory perception. If you want to see how it works just once, that won't scare you. What the interpreter does is mostly think of a place, near or far, for instance if people in Spain or in Belgium were requested to be seen using the Holy Spirit to guide him there, the person or people thought about would appear. The vision will be clear, but you'll know they are somewhere else than in your own presence. If you'd like to visit relatives on this side, sort of like snooping on them, you'd concentrate on their image first. What is he or she doing? Look for your siblings or friends clothing to appear too. Let's see what the Holy Spirit has to add in to help you along with out of body traveling to places you most desire.

The Lord says, "Penetrate smooth orange light through your mind first." Prayer would assist you. The Lord's pressing His hands together, which means that praying will help bring you to the destiny you're thinking of to see people after you've left your body, using what many wouldn't think of as "spiritual eyesight." To the interpreter it doesn't matter where he goes when he leaves his body, because he knows that he is still intact while sitting in place, physically. The orange light may linger on inside afterwards. Just bring it in straight through the back of your neck to where you believe the drawn spiritual beam to be helping you think better. Look straight ahead and think of who you want to see.

Now we will go deep inside of the Lord's kingdom, but if you prefer to do something else, then go right ahead. It's a daily routine for many of us "light workers" to enjoy receiving and giving spiritual messages while we purposely send ourselves into the light for joy, peace and happiness. "White tulips to help you feel at ease," Jesus says, while a golden sparkle appears. Jesus remembers the technique used where we place our thumbs together while facing our fingers up to the heavens for a good view. He is doing it too. He wants you to look for His tulips. Use the method. Didn't people in Hollywood do that with their hands when sizing up new potential stars for the silver screen? Yes they did, but you won't need to twist your hands all around, just center them slightly beneath your eyes. Rounding your fingers into a heart or into the shape of a small loaf of bread might help too. It is silly. The Lord thinks that you will think that.

There are many splendid ways to see on the other side of life. Those beautiful flowers are still fresh in the interpreter's mind, and someone just gently laid a long stem tulip upon a white covered alter. A gleaming gold cross sends warm light upon two leaves, whereas the beautiful flower is very thick and created white. "You were placed on this earth to be an inspiration to people," Jesus is telling your's truly. "I do just the opposite at times, Lord," response to the Lord's message. "That's true," He quickly answered. So it's time you were being told the truth on a continuing basis.

A bare chested heavyset tribesman is standing next to his double. His twin is much skinnier. The tribesman was some kind of special chief. His hair was quite tangled looking, no offense. In heaven with the "new look" his dark hair is much straighter to his shoulders and shinier. The change did him some good, although we can't really say he had a bad life on earth when he was here. All people are capable of love. "You say things like a true friend," he sends in visible words that come out of the air like magic. "You're not skeptical just curious," the man relates as the interpreter evaluates him very much. "We lived in the mountains at one point of time," he is saying. A silverfish was speared, and he's showing that he took a bite from it when attached to near the tip. "We ate fresh fish," he mentions. You can't get anything any fresher than that straight from the water. "I'm going to leave now," he said. He was thanked through prayer for visiting inside of the Holy Spirit. He really caused a happy chuckle. He made a whole silverfish take the place of the one that had a chunk taken out from it. Also, the friendly man gave considerable effort in bending his knees to leap up inside the light. He then smiled, and it was huge. Messaging suggested he wanted you to look at his life twice.

Just some of the blueness to heaven's spirit effuses over a dark boulder that has strands of bright sunlight across the hard layer to it. The visible boulder has a message printed across the front blending in through the front. And now between two sunlight rays of light the word "peace" was presented. The gold cross is in accord. Four golden hills are rising, but not lost from sight. A strong river of eternal silver waves of light flow past the sight, where two tall dark mountains in the foreground make it appear as though we are above them while rising to a new occasion.

"Your feelings are very intuitive when it comes to hidden peril," Jesus sends in a message. Not to frighten anyone, there are two automobiles the Lord is making us aware of in a vision. They have crashed and sit at a dead stop on different angles. The Lord says, "You may be warned in dreams or spiritual visions of an accident." That should feel "special" to feel intuitive with warnings happening. "Our side knows your feelings about money," comes through now. They are not kidding us, they do know everything about us. It can have a crippling effect on many not having enough to spend. We will be too busy to be thinking about money in heaven.

About the baseball player and helmeted football player sitting at a fancy white table, where an entrance is nearby them with swirling black posts, and decorated walls with golden sparkly flowers and small crosses upon them, it's a peaceful place in heaven where they are committed to signing autographs. That's right it's helpful for people in heaven to still believe that much interest has been given with playful activity. A young boy with brown eyes is delighted to have his baseball and glove signed. Signatures in dark writing appear with him holding onto both. He's a funny boy. Most of the child from head to toe is of all white light. He could be any nationality. The message ended. Enough said now.

Someone from inside of the spirit world is playing peekaboo. "I really enjoy life," the Lord says as He stands here in the spirit. The Lord's violet blossoms released from heaven touch the floor of earth, and when looking back at Him one of the smaller but gentle flowers laid gently upon His nose. "I'm concerned for your well-being," Jesus interjects. A sharp blue and white streak of eternal light darts across the floor. Do you see it too? A message of harmony. A piece of brown toast sticking out of a toaster and the words "to you" was something spiritual to solve. The easy spiritual message in the light. A tall silver chalice with sizzling white light above the rim was raised to the Lord's lips, causing the interpreter to become jarred. Jesus then moved His hand quickly back and forth to His mouth twice. He is taking this celebration of toasting His people to a new level. The chalice just grew about three feet high. The Lord says, "I celebrate being in your company." Nodding in agreement here, and a little bit of His warm vibrations of light were felt. "You're equal to them," Jesus says, while the interpreter silently thought about who was more important to toast, the people in heaven or those of us here on earth.

It is time to see what else they want to show you. The spirit suddenly loops. "Don't forget we love you," special people from the afterlife have spoken. It really was from them. They also feel it was appropriate to give a message more immediately. Who could they be? Let's take a gander. A big woman who is seated wearing a flower print on her dress wants someone reading to acknowledge her. "Please excuse my intrusion on your life," the polite lady expresses. She is more than welcome to visit, it's her heaven. "My granddaughter knows I am well now," with spoken words. But who is she? She said, "The month of June is when I departed." Whoever this very lovely is she holds a sweet bouquet of white flowers in her hands and places one over a gravestone. "My children would acknowledge this too," she explains while adjusting her hands. She holds out her hand. "I still wear my wedding ring," was relayed in a mental message. She's still spiritual. She is now gliding through the spirit seated, but gracefully and not like some sort of race car driver.

A very bright spark of gold eternal light shines on the top of a rounded halo. That too is gold, but at a much lower coloring. Does the sparkle continue blinking off and on or was that just a one time occurrence to get our attention focused on to the light? The golden dashes of light inside of the Lord's hands brighten upon them. That light was released from His left hand into the spirit, over his head, to where it stopped in intervals to brighten. The full thicker halo wasn't there though. Three golden stars were perfected over the Lord's head now. He is fast, but patient. Sure enough there they are, two more gold stars glittering, one by each ear. A total of five, except that the stars next to His ears were tiny. They were actually shinier.

That fourteen inch high tall dark red rose that just disappeared didn't leave a scent in the air, but it has been said that sometimes the aromas do fill the air, from unnatural sights sensed from the other side. Shaped like a car but a little longer, people are excited about the ride they are taking inside of one. "It will feel like you are gliding and floating at the same time," a woman mentions after throwing her head back gently in all of the excitement. One strange thing was, though, she is holding onto a steering wheel where a strip of golden light is beaming over her hands. "We are in control of where we want to go," she says. The ride isn't restrictive in movement, not at all. It would remind you of a shuttle if you rode it.

Let's watch her go about her merry way. "I'm a light traveler too," she mentions. The clarity of white light for windows is quite interesting and non-breakable. "We will pass my favorite areas now," she shares with us. That's too unbelievable, but here we go. The Lord interjects, "It's true but you will have to prove that she is traveling in the light with you." She is passing in front of a huge cathedral with many high, waxy white arched windows. Small white angels and the baby Jesus are surrounded by glowing golden light penetrating through a few areas of the windows up high. The lady inside of the transport vehicle is in awe. She presses her hands against her face while looking up to the breathtaking view. One of the tall windows has brightened in white at the top, but the rest of the window down below has a long edge of baby blue light seeping through a strip of smooth white light. At the bottom sits a bouquet of red roses with a big black and silver glittering bow around the stems. That same woman who brought us here is sitting inside a smooth white light surrounding her ride. Hard telling if someone has lost their marbles but here goes. The labeled "play" button, and the word "music" appears inside of her vehicle with a golden musical note floating around. It's not a real car, but some sort of heavenly invention for her and all other people able and willing to soar through the heavens in.

She is almost ready to appear again. The interpreter lost track of where she was inside of the light, but the Lord shined through twice. She says, "I can see you are a worrier about money." That's a bad habit and she is spot on. Well the word "Faith" came in now. There's pink framework everywhere like never seen before inside of her spirit world.

The dimensions are many is why. Our tour guide has finally shown herself more outside of all the spotless white light. Her hair is full of waves down to her shoulders. The huge white angels sweeping through the spirit give so much peace that they have sidetracked our attention some to where we were heading to with the lady. It will be interesting to visit the next favorite place.

"You didn't think that I could return," our tour guide relates in a flash. She quickly turns left to smell a single violet, and over to the right is where she demanded our attention to another violet. She smelled both as they remain in mid-air inside the spiritual energy of a dimension of holy light. "Do you think that we forgot about how you adore such pets?" she asked with the amazing sight of a Dachshund with her pups nearby. Inside of the light you can expect anything new to happen too. You know something? Nothing is impossible with God.

He has the biggest brown eyes you have ever seen. They are twice the normal size and so are His eyelashes. That was Him here in the spirit. He looked like Jesus with the beard and mustache and long hair. Naturally He will change, even the color in His eyes. He just showed big blue eyes too. His eyes are warm and He crouched over some when gliding in through the spirit. Is He ever someone special or what? So very loving is the look inside of His tender eyes, you'd swear you were looking at a bearded child with extra large eyes. That's silly we know already how weird it sounded, but those eyes. We can come back to the lady with her magic transport vehicle in a minute, she knows what's happening with the Lord and God. The interpreter has to see God. Relaxing in the comfort of the spiritual world's peaceful presence, curiosity of where God could have gone is getting the better part of the interpreter. But what did appear was a baby elephant with those same brown eyes. Usually elephants do not have such enlarged eyes as these.

How about the lion's head poking in through white light with huge brown eyes now? God is doing this with His animals from inside of the kingdom. The lion is half white and half golden. God and the Lord are being supremely funny right now. A donkey kept appearing, and suddenly that animal was sitting on its rear-end upon a white throne. Then a word message came from our Father in heaven. "Wouldn't it be unusual to see that in heaven?" He said. "It does already!" exclaimed the interpreter in prayer. "You would like me to comment," the Holy Spirit responded. "It's up to you, God," said back. "I am your heavenly Father," He says, as gold sparkles were given in the open air from God as a way to show He is real. While wondering about the pretty lady touring heaven, God sent a worded message stating, "She awaits your return." Funny that message came in twice actually, because the interpreter after seeing it once about her, it had been forgotten about what God had mentioned beforehand. But, God came through and showed the message again in the softest golden wording you've ever seen. He has a way of helping you feel good, like you were walking around on vacation in heaven without a care in the world.

"I find that Father God was helpful to you," our lovely assistant was saying. She plucked a yellow tulip from the heavens and slid it inside of her hair over to the left side. She says, "I have one for you too." It is half poppy and half white. She twirls the flower ever so slowly to show off her talent of how she has mastered the art of the mystique. The flower is slowly turning a soft hue of pink where there is white. After smelling the wonderful aroma she begins twirling the flower faster, so fast that the flower's petals have red pinstripes. "What do you think just happened then?" she asked while pointing to the white flower in her hair. That's right she changed it from yellow to all white now. We give up on how that happened and maybe she will tell us. "The light penetrated inside of the flower's petals to change the color," she says. Watching her present these words, and determining if she is saying what she is telling us is truthful is a big job. More of that "non-belief" factor seeps in now and then. Then when the message is told twice, when in doubt, it is then the right time for all good men to go back to work again. That holds true in the case of the interpreter vocalizing what should be told.

If you are down and out think of good changes coming soon. A thin waxy white pointer is pointing to the sunshine in a smaller size. Definitely a spiritual person helping. Look on the bright side of things. "Your mind is expected to grow with literature," the spirit world announces, relaying it to the interpreter and the people. A large sandaled foot is ready to either land flat or has been stepping to the sound of music. The word "music" was shown in print. Now is He or She, Jesus and God or Mary? Hard telling yet, only one raised foot in the spirit world was glanced at. You need to believe what is going to be said to you. While expecting to see someone a guest did arrive. That foot and feet belong to the Lord. He did something new to speak of for the time being. He stood in calm white light with both feet levitated off the ground, as He is inside of the spirit world, and the Lord had His arms crossed, a perfect example of superior levity happening. All spiritual people must really love following His lead. Not only do the magical swamis and gurus levitate in the spirit, we all will. Before this slips away the experience must be shared with everyone paying close attention today.

The interpreter tries staying in the background at times when it comes to messaging, but it's just getting too impossible to do. While driving down the street today in the forest city, the Lord came out of the blue to disclose His closeness in spirit, so up front with Himself that He was seen standing at least four stories high. This was outdoors in public, and He was giant! As tall and wonderful as a good King could be, that's our Lord. "I can do that for anyone who asks," Jesus is saying now. You'll never forget the day He appears before you. You won't have time to say much, there's a peaceful feeling though, no denying you'll feel the oneness suddenly. The words "Peaceful and Jesus" appeared in the air. The Lord says, "I'm not disturbed by your actions, you just need discipline." And folded prayer hands rest upon an open Bible. Then pressed prayer hands point up to God, also with golden light upon them.

Praise the Lord and God. And thank you, Virgin Mary. "I am here with you," the Virgin Mary said with the look of so much love upon Her face. Her head was bowed a little, her soft lips curling slightly on the right side, to let you know She can be warm in heaven. The interpreter, looking up to Her, waiting on Mary to open Her eyes more, they are moving slowly and beautiful blue eyes become wide open, and Mary's smile brings one about from seeing how loving

She really is. "Thank you, Mary. Mary, you certainly are beautiful," complimented in prayer to when seeking Her out even more. "I am helping you," She says sweetly, when words appeared in the air with Her conveying them. Now the interpreter feels like a kid in a candy store waiting for a really good treat. What if She has returned to help everyone else too? Why that's alright it's expected. She says, "Be very cautious with them." Meaning everybody and everyone. She was asked, "Mary, what is that covering your head?" While smelling a very small pink flower with light white to its edge, Mary said, "Use your intuitive side." When trying to understand what else Mary would say, concerning the covering over Her hair an answer was finally received. "Tell them it is a holy shroud from Jesus," speaking words of wisdom from the other side of life. Gold and white light created the cross upon Her soft shroud. The Bible is in Her presence and Mary says, "You should know more about the good book." A beautiful fanning gold halo just filled in over Mary's head with good size ivory wings springing up behind Mary, and a white glow came beneath Her right underarm. You kind of wonder if Mary will be hesitant at giving more messages, or if She happened to have ascended back through the heavens.

Two rounded off silver crosses have much glistening borders around them. They are across from each other, and now it is time to see what else has been brought about to light. "Both are little ones," the Holy Spirit announces about the kids with their arms wrapped around the crosses. The boy on the right has a white halo with a golden cross inside. "My mother is where you are," the little girl expresses using words. And the earth appeared too. Her halo was golden with a white cross on top. Both of the children have white wings that overlap the rounded edges to their crosses. The spirit believes we have the right idea. The Holy Spirit says, "Wait until you know for sure." Messaging will commence. Many oval white eggs become larger as each one comes through the light. The last one showed is where a baby chick remains sitting still inside of the cracked shell. Bright gold light shines upon the baby chick. The little boy is smiling and hands the yellow chick to the girl from hand to hand. The baby chick's small wings are spreading, and strangely enough the next sight was of a very smooth white angel embedding the baby chick inside of her own wings.

Why would the Lord be cringing in pain with His right cheek becoming indented? He is here, make no mistake about it, when He appears bearded with long hair and mustache, that's Jesus! Now He moved His head off to the right, laying His pressed together prayer hands against His cheek. He is sending us a spiritual message, alerting us to pray to Him when we are in pain. Inner depth of the interpreter's mind, he was wondering if the Lord could show brown light. Without notice the Lord created two swaths of brown light, just what was being thought of. That's hard to believe, right? The Lord says, "I would question that too." The brown light made an "equal" sign.

"Don't question, just dictate the message," Jesus insisted upon. Too much judging is why the Lord said what He did. Everything He and His Father and Mary reveal are for a reason. A gigantic black sail swept through the spirit seeming a little out of control. It had thinned out considerably. If there's a ship it wasn't visible, but a solid black ball was beneath the sail. Studying the Holy Spirit the sail turns completely white and is fully operable. It has spread outward and gusts of wind fill the sail to move it on across blue waters. Now above the ship a circle of white light shines from a silver star presented as an symbol. A very slender yellow candle glows. Many white sails upon the seas, with a small spiritual boy cupping his hands around the candle is indicating the unification of sailors upon the sea. "Stay the course with the Lord," the Holy Spirit interjects. Who was this for? "Your ship is ready to come in," also from the spirit. Let's believe it is our ship and that we are well-deserving of any and all blessings coming our way now. Jesus prefers that it is for you too. He had secretly related that to the interpreter, and it was decided upon "not to judge," but to include everyone else along with himself with that message of hope.

The Holy Spirit seems to be saying, "So there!" The sudden sharp movements in the light relate as such, and that's pretty much on the money. The Holy Spirit shows a penny, therefore assuming that's what God meant. Ever believe you have seen God in your sleep or in a very holy vision? He can look Ancient Roman, sitting there proudly on His throne with a floor length majestical robe. This is cool. Of the Lord's dynasty a royal figure holding up a large bunch of white grapes before His mouth, nibbles on one. He resembles Jesus, facially, but His dark hair is quite jagged across the front of His forehead. He has a long white robe on. Attached to His robe is a velvety black garment that's draped across His right shoulder. One of the Romans from earlier times? "Not exactly a Roman emperor," the Holy Spirit responds. Transparent angels of the light stretch their wings out with one at each side of His throne. He sits upon the throne peering upward as rays of golden light shine like two suns from the sky. He says, using black lettering to create words, "My name is Father God." Okay with Him over here. Looking up to Him for answers, He doesn't bombard the interpreter with a super humongous spiritual light or unusual vision, they are ordinary, a gold flash, some aquamarine colors of heaven and variations of red and pink flowers. One which was the red, that He holds dearly to Himself in front of His nose. "Ask for guidance," the Holy Spirit announces. What in the world? A bunch of gorgeous white flowers tied together with a black bow have a tinge of golden light beautifying them.

No way did he just come in through the spirit. Salvador Dali, that's who he is. No, the interpreter wasn't wrong. That huge twisty mustache and contented look on his face is from his good nature. Maybe he did have a mysterious look in his eyes and on his face when alive as a famous painter. He seems more relaxed especially told from the soft lips and smile upon his face. No tension whatsoever. Waiting to see him again for a message. Or was that it of how he feels in heaven now? He says, "Speak my name." And he was standing next to a canvas painting. "I want them to see that I love my painting still," he relates. The interpreter still finds it hard to believe he can interpret spiritual messages from famous people too. When Salvador first came in he was really vivid. "Many famous artists are here with me," he is saying, while some of them can be seen with puffy black artist's hats on. He wants us to try a little bit of artwork in the future.

This is what he showed on the canvas leaning against the easel. With white in the background, the foreground reveals the backhand

and fist of someone's hand with the index finger pointing up. That would be someone's right hand. The famous artist is using his brush to lightly touch the tip of the index finger with gold paint. At least the finger sparkles now. Salvador is really smiling big, and there's so much golden light around him it is just from out of this world and into the next. Wait until you're there on that side of life. He said, "They won't think it's real, when the interpreter was ready to bring Picasso in too." But, Picasso just appeared and he says, "Hi!" Unbelievable, but what a real joy to view them, how blessed they are, and how very fortunate we are to know the Lord and God can enlighten us with such famous artists. Whether we are with them on earth or in heaven, they have become welcome by the general public, many who are big art lovers.

Now there are those two guys again, this time Salvador and Picasso are side by side, but only their faces were visible high up in the air. Remember, the interpreter is here on earth, therefore, the Holy Spirit and our airspaces are very significant, where these messages, and images appear, and where spiritual people from the other side of life live and breathe within. Dali was on Picasso's right side, and they are so close, almost cheek to cheek. Picasso's face just turned a very soft blue color from holy light in front of him now. He turned away from Dali and was enjoying much more comfort from the light of God. "Tell them to visualize Picasso in blue light," a secret message appears. It's could have been secretive to the interpreter if he feels there are some doubters inside of the public eye. The Holy Spirit just related, "You're not afraid to express yourself when it comes to messages." Picasso says, "He's like Einstein a little bit." He could be relating that about the man who is reading this. One last thing about Picasso. He is so funny appearing inside of the Holy Spirit right now with a soft, bright swath of orange light in the form of a mustache that formed across his upper lip. It has to do with an image mostly. Perhaps the reason why the colorful mustache didn't curl up on the ends was because of the artist not wanting to fully imitate his painter pal. What a sense of humor. Will they ever show their faces again? When you arrive in heaven, don't worry you'll see them. The desires of your heart will be fulfilled in the Lord's presence.

A candelabrum with all white flowers have small flames that were orange, blue and even gold. Wait a minute now it isn't a repeat in heaven, it's for blessing two small children facing them on their knees. They're really cute so humble in the Lord's spirit. The brown haired children's hair have swirled around in front of their foreheads. Pink cheeks of flawlessness. The girl holds her left hand to her ear. She wants us to listen. Between the children and the Lord using this method to gain our utmost attention, they've become profoundly helpful in our growth. These kids are too saintly not to be seen by the readers. And the interpreter is going to gain one hundred percent spiritual knowledge on how to bring them in close so everyone will have a chance to see the candelabrum, and both children on bended knee. "Look at me," the small girl says.

She wrapped a small gold and silver bow around her index finger so you could at least see her. "Tell them I'm living in heaven," she says. Her sleeve is an off white color but spectacular to see. Look for a small ruffle near her wrist. The bow may brighten too. If you can't look up near your ceiling somewhere, into the light, where you'll be able to see the little boy in his white robe praying to the Lord, then you will need to pray to see him to sharpen your intuition. Just plain wow! They say in the light, "The readers will think it's crazy the way you think." That has been thought all along though, so no worries here in the interpreter's corner.

"Love your brothers and sisters in the spirit of God and the Lord," said from the Lord's words appearing and by His special visitation. The Lord's hands covered in white light reach forward, and as they have opened and lay flat, one by one three whiter candles appeared on a simple pathway in life, that which the Lord and His Father have given us to follow them upon. It was an idea to ask God to bring in more famous people within spirituality of the Holy Spirit. The Lord told the interpreter, "Don't force your ideas on them." But, that doesn't mean the Lord and God won't be surprising us with other influential guests of spirit form. The Holy Spirit can be very effectual. What is the vision of pouches for any ways? This message won't be hard to decipher.

Three tan color pouches come to view in heaven. The Holy Spirit have three kangaroos front and center, two in front of the adorable creature in the back. No way is anyone going to believe the Lord is doing what He is displaying to the interpreter. "That's really sweet Lord," the interpreter tells the Lord in a prayer. The Lord hasn't disappeared with His furry creatures nearby. Jesus hugs one of the long eared kangaroos from behind. His arms wrapped around, him or her, so lovingly. And you know what? The Lord's vibration of light moves so light-heartedly that it isn't hard to tell that Jesus is chuckling. Purple blue shades of light delight.

"You need more understanding of the spirit," Jesus tells us. Instantly white flowers glow in front of the yellow tulip. "I have my reasons for so many visions of flowers," He relates to us. We will be involved in many fun events that will require concentration inside of the kingdom of God. You will be asked if you love the Lord too. Your answers to His questions will always be good. Don't worry about your journey. A small boy skims his left hand upon a small amount of silvery water in heaven. He holds up a silver fish that seems to have a yellow teardrop falling from its eye. Quickly the boy releases the fish with swishing it back into the water now. Interesting if anything at all. "I can fish here," the boy says. He held onto a huge golden reel, but the rest of his pole wasn't visible. His speech pattern inside of visible words was though.

A few golden vibrations of soft light rolls across the floor, nearing the interpreter now. Across from each other small white fish appear, almost tail to tail, but not touching each other in the light. Each fish has a small golden halo. Not weird, but that's what the interpreter thought for a minute down here on earth. Two pretty black and blue striped fish are farther away, facing each other. A black wedge between all of the fish leads to a gold circle of light where they are headed to now. They have all glided into the Lord's hands which are in the "giving" manifestation.

Colorful hearts come in and highlight the message. "You are in our hearts," sent to earth. A steep avalanche of snow falls violently downward. A man is skiing as fast as he can very determined to beat the snow from burying him alive. He looks scared stiff still. Likely a strong premonition coming from above. In brighter golden lettering the message reads: He is a survivor. The avalanche with pretty white snow was quite a sight. The Lord did show him stuck inside of the snow with his head above the top of the mound. Even so the man did survive. However the Lord does mention saving people from snow mounds, whereas, when happening where death was apparent, the Lord's hands reach out with Him making gigantic mounds of snowfall look like a small amount. While reaching over it to lift people up into His arms for comfort life giving golden light is glowing everywhere. Two people with their snowsuit and gloves on can be seen inside of the light, hence, when they arrived in heaven they were dressed the same as when they were snow skiing. They have sort of learned their lesson about the danger in avalanches. It was said that they were males, but as they are being watched inside of the spirit world, it is now easily told they have changed into white robes with appreciable neat creasing. "Many others are here who have experienced the same," the Holy Spirit explains.

Colors make you wonder their meanings. Eventually we will have "full" knowledge of their denotation. At times we are shown words along side of color. We all know too well that blue is for the sky, but in heaven, "beauty upon the earth" is the true meaning. My God and good Lord! The Lord applauds the message with His right hand patting against His left. Let's see what He feels about "color." A caramel white vibration appeared near Him in the spirit world. Then two wings were formed. "I choose to comment on that," He wanted said. Four sets of wings encircle the Lord now. "I vow to be truthful to you," Jesus is actually sending words too.

"Because of the spirit you are able to venture into the light," well said. Some will think there has to be concrete proof to what He is saying. Have faith in the Lord and you will see the angels appear around His shoulders and front area. Seeming to be clinging onto Him. "If you believe in angels you should be able to see them too," Jesus is now telling us. And the Lord believes the interpreter should continue quoting what He is saying. "Excellent, good Lord," the interpreter speaks out to the Lord inside of His holy presence.

From the Lord's hands a baby dove lifts gently touching our air, but leaving the spirit world to fly softly in four levels, and reaching earth was also a simple task for Jesus to do. The gentleness of the gravitating dove with Jesus enabling the bird to fly and float was masterful. And Jesus is glad we acknowledge the dove of sacredness. A large white leaf appears with the wording reading: Palm Sunday. Was there really clothing laid in the holy pathway as well? "There were many gifts laid about for me," Jesus speaks out about the holy time in His life. Jesus is here with a thorn wreath upon Him. Enough to make one cry. "Blessed are thee who love the Lord," Jesus is speaking right now with dark lettered words again. "The crucifix was painful for me," He says. We should be glad that He has found a pleasant way to communicate through the interpreter today. Time is time until our day's have ended, but timelessness is eternity, and with life lasting forever in heaven the Lord's words will truthfully be spoken at a moment's notice.

The Lord and God and the Virgin Mary are mighty-mighty. A very long line at forty-five degrees, drawn out inside of the Holy Spirit led to a small black, upright candle, which has a bright yellow flame. It feels as though you have such beautiful insight moving around from the Lord that anything ordinary seems a bit immaterial, there's so much more beauty in heaven than here. The lady here was thought to be old fashion. Her hair curls are very long, meeting her shoulders. Brown and matching her eyes. Very pretty with short bangs, she spins her yellow and white umbrella around, then she stops abruptly. Small in her hands, but suddenly the umbrella flips over landing nearby the lady where it became ten times the size it was when she handled her belonging. "I feel like a fairy princess," she says. The white patterns in her dress are very soft. The umbrella's handle is sticking up in the heavens as very ivory with white light on the end. She has a red apple with shiny golden leaves attached to it. A first for everything.

Sparkling gold light the size of a twinkling star enlightens. She is holding onto a sparkling gold heart that you can see-through. You'd swear she was steering the heart like at a wheel. Holding it up close to her face, now she certainly didn't need to prove herself being here, coming from the exquisite heavens to entertain you, but she did by looking straight through from the other side of life, a woman of all heart. "You are very special people," she says up close. Inside of her dear heart she was able to deliver God's messages. Inside of a baby blue light Jesus stands toe-toe with someone. The spiritual man with Him is noble and He is moving His fingers rapidly as though He were typing now. Or is He trying to tell the Interpreter to keep on with the good work using his hands? Piano keys now appeared with gold light flashing over them. Unknown why yet, but the upper black "sharp," and a singular lower piano key becomes very large. A glistening golden key was just laid upon it. The Lord wants everyone, including the interpreter, to evaluate what He has given us. "I invite you into my castle," Jesus just poured out into words from that golden throne, which "your's truly" has the pleasure of seeing.

A question for God. We appreciate all walks of life, their nationality and color of skin, but were there more than one Adam and Eve? "My son, I am the beginning and ending of all," said in the spirit. "What do you mean by ending of all, God?" the interpreter asked. "In your time the ending will come," He says through this special rendering. That clarified what was on the interpreter's mind. "How about Adam and Eve though?" asked. "They did live earlier in life," is the message sent within mild golden light. The spirit of God is known. "You are inquisitive today," God messages. You can't get any closer than that through prayer and meditation. Well perhaps you will. The Holy Spirit is saying, "Your gift is prophecy." Above a large white gift box those words appeared. The baby blue ribbon is special. We have the gift.

"I feel for you," Jesus is saying in the spirit to someone. "Thank you," were words returned to the Lord. But, they weren't given from the interpreter, only seen as to what the conversation was all about in heaven. A streak of orange penetrates the heavens. "My life was good, Jesus," a lady basking in holy white light explains to the Lord. It appears she has just passed on into the light and the Lord is sharing her new experience in life with us. The Lord's very colorful peachy complexion is something to be admired. The interpreter doesn't think he has ever seen Jesus this close before, and so colorful. He makes you want to behave and feel good at the same time. Jesus says, "It's okay to say." Jesus was firmly holding a small bunch of baby breath flowers in His hand. And you know something else? There is a lady with the Lord whom He has given the arrangement of lovely white flowers. These visitations go really well with the sounds of rushing waters over rocky surfaces, if you can only envision that in your mind. The Lord is showing water making its way between several rocks of various sizes.

Funny as it seems three pink french horns appear on an angle. The word "sessions" appeared too. There are various colors with them likely to help in feeling spirited. An elevated tall pink candle is glowing, but mostly in a wide band of whiteness. White footwear will be offered to wear while you are in heaven. "One of many gifts to receive," the Lord related. They do look very soft and comfortable. No more worries about sore feet. When four narrow blue candles appear in the spirit world, they offer hope and some help to people, and they are the Lord's creation. "Be still my son," the Lord says to the interpreter, while sitting here anticipating the heavens to open up much more than they have. Unbelievable, just unbelievable.

Not more than seven feet away a fluffy white bird's feather bends, and the face of a young Indian man appears. "The spirit moves softly when with you," he mentions. The slice of rock attached to his small war club is interesting. The word "wrong" comes through. The interpretation is correct, it's just a reminder of wartime being inappropriate. He holds a glowing yellow candle in his left hand. Now the interpreter isn't so tired of seeing candles after all. It is too bad that more appreciation isn't given to God's marvelous visions and out of body experiences, then more enjoyment would follow from being a little more in accordance with them. Many dark rooftops with smoking chimneys have now turned all white top. You wouldn't trade having the light of God and His Son in your life.

Uplifting inside of the Holy Spirit. "Lord, we need to see great things in the spirit," spoken for in prayer. "Ask and it shall be given,"

Jesus replied. Should we ask again? "I will help you," He said right off the bat. An arched golden gate bridge lights up in heaven, not on our side. The interpreter was afraid something bad may happen to the Golden Gate in America, but that was a real mistake. The words, "Not Serious" appeared as is. The bridge in heaven is sparkling and very grand. From a window in heaven a woman tends to a box of white flowers hanging outside on the ledge. Surprisingly her back is to the interpreter as she is taking in the view of the golden trestle a distance away now. Heaven is unusual where you can see through everything at will.

A white sheet is held onto at its end with someone's hands discernible. The sheet began sliding over a person and it did cover someone's head. Not something enjoyable to watch, or anything we would really want to hear about. Ivory angels form a v-shape around the body and soul. "What happened?" a woman asks in the light as she has been transformed immediately while wearing angelic wings. "I am sorry for your loss," Jesus says with the deepest sympathy afforded to His people. Jesus is so kind and He comes in through the spirit. "Your friend has passed on," He mentions too. Exactly what the interpreter was afraid of, and sadly enough tears flow. Suspected all along. Obviously it was sort of personal, a situation a little unsure of. Many signs have been forthcoming. Time to let the complex situations rest for now. "You have a friend in her," a message from the Lord about one of the interpreter's friends.

"The time is nigh for the Lord to come," sworn to God and to the Virgin Mary, that their Father, who art in heaven had sent forth this message inside of the Holy Spirit. It seems like there was something important to do. That's one way of avoiding the subject of passing over. On with transcribing things human beings would find hard to deem possible.

"The Holy Spirit is extremely proud of you on this day," Jesus conveys. Brilliance of blue and white light drops from the heavens beautifully. The angel babies are back and seen even clearer. There are at least six kiddies inside of soft orange-white clouds, individually riding in their own to behold. Golden t-shape guide sticks for them to handle for steering with. A small girl with spruced up blonde hair gives the "victory" sign while saying, "Hi." Noticeably there were two blue wings popping up pointing outward in back of her. The interpreter didn't do a double or triple take, if there's anything such as a "four-take" to be taken it was just accomplished. The Lord is inside of a soft white vibration that's actually clear, to where His own personal white angel behind Himself is taking care of the many children, by touching them gently, guiding each child, and the very vibrant white light shining upon each one of His little ones reflects friendship and love from their very devoting Savior and friend. As big as Jesus is, and as small as His children are it is so extra special to be watching Jesus speaking to these children with the children's faces so close to His, obviously as they relate back and forth. "My children are my world too," Jesus says. They would like in depth analysis of the light.

The Lord's right foot treads through sand now. That's what He is doing in the Holy Spirit to prove Himself. There is a real scorpion near His foot. "I am aware you believe in my walk of life," Jesus conveyed. He is speaking. "My message was conveyed similar," He believes. Large and small pink candy cane hooks are interspersed. One tinier pink cane is wrapped into the end of a ruffled white wing. Why so cute? Because if the interpreter was a betting man, he'd think that an angel was either going to give it to someone or there was going to be magic made now. The cane just turned all gold, and brother does it ever glitter. It wouldn't matter if you were lame or not, you'd be proud to walk the streets with that baby. You'd be the richest man or woman on earth with that. It is nice to see a glowing gold hand with the gentleman or gentlewoman displaying a baby blue egg in whoever's hand it's in. We need to find out who. The egg is sparkly gold all over now. But where did that person's hand go, besides their entire self? By the way, the robin's egg was oversized. Now it's a marvel to see, especially at Easter time which is nearing now. A white cross glows. Picture a small blue egg and a large one. The Lord thinks they'll appear around the lower area where you are situated at.

"I was confined before my passing," Jesus is relating right now. Thank you Jesus! "My Mother thinks you are a special person," relating that to you too. A huge golden flash almost stunned the interpreter. You have to stop and ask yourself, was I just in heaven? More of the kind of question regarding leaving earth for good, ending up in a different dimension for real. It felt good. The spiritual side of life and sensation of heaven's light is enough to make you want to get up and boogie. Or maybe a waltz. "Just let us in to heaven when you are ready," expressed openly. Now that's feeling good about passing on over, and by the way, our Lord knew what kind of experience it would be for Him too.

'Begin telling the truth," the Lord highly suggested from His throne. Yes, and the Lord has those nice ivory wings, and the white robe which is very appealing. He is looking down as if His main attention is focused in on His very stomach area. He had mentioned about being "mean-spirited," how it only hurts yourself. "Soldiers have bowed down before me during the resurrection," said. Jesus is in time for our Passover, our Good Friday, and for another wonderful time of the year, Easter. This is why you have heard what He had spoken moments ago. We can only thank Jesus. He feels it is very thoughtful to be thinking of Him. "Pray for relief," He says in the spirit.

Why wonder about mounting head tension, just pray when He says to. Or when you have much needed relief. "Praise the Lord, I could use some relief right now," the interpreter spoke to the Lord with a calm prayer. Maybe others could use our Lord's help first. That was secretly mentioned to the Lord in prayer. You know what? Heal! That is what the Lord will do for your pain, especially after asking for others to be tended to. "Why did the Lord just send that warm healing vibration to me?" the interpreter asked himself inside. After giving serious thought about the lame and many of the helpless souls in the universe, there was little doubt afterwards, that the Lord can show you how He can heal anyone, anywhere, at anytime of the day or night.

Praise the Lord. Here we go into a new direction, one you should enjoy very much indeed. "I have visited you in the womb," Jesus coveys using visible wording. He felt we would be surprised in life by the many wonders. Jesus is very understanding of how we feel about His interest in our new beginnings in life. A lot of white light is softly glowing upon a woman's belly as the Lord is by her side. "Helpers are tending to the children in heaven for a reason," Jesus said, while many small ones are aided by women wearing folded white hats. Life seems so important, especially on their side. An infant being held has a squeeze toy that's very golden with four rounded sides. "There are many health issues in life," Jesus says. One of the best messages ever. "I cherish autistic children," Jesus said, as He comes inside of the earthly plane in His Holy Spirit. A beautiful purple-blue angelic presence arrived with a woman. The angelic robe had smaller wings, but the robe, which is smoother than the finest and smoothest silk was far-out and heavy. "You'll like our ways when you come here," she says in a special language which the interpreter knows is of God. Sensitive pink light caresses her eyelids, those which have lowered slightly, on account of the lady with the wings wanting to help us understand that the existence of light is beautiful. "You're going to cry now," are words spelled out in the Holy Spirit. But why will that happen? "Your mother might be the angel here," Jesus must be sending that message. The interpreter is hesitant to shed tears, only because it is likely that the Lord might be referring to "others" who may shed a tear because of the spiritual lady of white light upon her face. That robe and wings are really choice. A hint about the angelical lady. Her hair was curled up on the ends, almost meeting her shoulders. There is something you should be told.

So far a woman sitting at a golden harp strumming away at her song and much movement of the Holy Spirit shaping a slide or backside to another angel arrived. Two butterscotch tulips fill the air, but don't see them in your mind in a dark shade. They were very light in hue. "I cleanse thee with light," Jesus seems to be saying. Blue and silver sparkle together, only moments after viewing people on the other side bathing in the spreading, glorious white which we may yearn to partake with them one day when we arrive. It sort of sounds like a rundown of what's to come and it is. Then why such overwhelming sadness if we are to be expected in this next life to be overwhelmed with tremendous happiness? Some people are doubtful that they will be happy again. "I can help you feel better," are words appearing now.

This will be interesting receiving the interpretation for the yellow foot with a thin black outline around each toe. Then again, will the Lord tell us that His words are printed inside of the Holy Spirit as real?

"Speak my words," Jesus conveyed now. A three foot white angel with matching halo is holding a bouquet of colorful flowers. Someone inside of the angelic presence takes a whiff of them. One at a time the yellow and white flowers are picked from the bunch and become suspended in mid-air, including a bright red rose. In the background, the Lord rests upon His throne in absolute peace of where everybody is in heaven, but you really need to look for Him, because so many people have placed flowers before Him that it looks like a colossal flower shop. "Do the best you can with them," Jesus says, but it was uncertain if that should have been disclosed. The things seeming maybe not important really are after all.

A golden drawbridge. A long pathway stretches near and far, somewhere where we will be able to experience life's adventures. A path in heaven, because that golden drawbridge was a materialistic object on the earthly plane becoming visible like that. A black treasure chest opens and one gold nugget was pocketed, but you could see through it. Having x-ray eyes, right? It works that way in heaven. The message about gold and searching for knowledge inside of the Lord's light becomes the answer in analogy. Pressed together prayer hands in the spirit with a gold nugget near them. Go ahead and pray for knowledge, or if you feel lucky, ask to be blessed with gold from the kingdom of God. A swirling golden tray appears with a golden cross in the middle. It tilts forward, and the person responsible for moving it around shows that the cross stays in mid-air inside of heaven, when the tray was removed. A gold sparkle along with a golden overelaborate love seat appears. But the Lord knows no limits. He has guaranteed we would have the very best life with Him in the afterlife. The Lord is sitting upon this beautiful furnishing along side of a woman who is excited about seeing the interpreter. Jesus admires her with His face turned to her. The interpreter thought that it might be a little bit too much to hear, but here goes. The interpreter's aunt appears next to the Lord, and she says, using visible words, "I'm really at ease now." You know how when you have your visual contact with the other side and family visits with you, everything is much real, that's enough to make you think how lucky you are. Family is safe and sound, and look just by the latest example of how all-purpose our Lord makes Himself to all of us. He is very leisure able. Stripes of pink, yellow and white light glow. But the Lord's face and crown are seen inside of a whiter light now. He is very high with God.

Now it can told. An actual ruler and glowing gold opening of a tunnel connect. The Lord is the "Ruler." He says, "I am amazed." Jesus would appreciate it if the image of a bitten into apple and the visitors, "man and woman" inside white light were communicated openly about who they are and why they've come to us. "Adam and Eve were thought to have been their names," the Holy Spirit relates. A beautiful garden with twirling vines and colorful flowers were created all around them. "There is a grain of truth concerning them," Jesus sends in an instant message from heaven. They were led into a garden by the Holy Spirit. The young man, he has a determined look on his face, and believe it or not his right hand pressed against his side. We are on track.

He says, "Tell them woman was created from my rib cage." A little at first he was confused when coming into the world. "I was made in the perfect image of our Father who art in heaven," he sent in a message. Small but very beautiful golden segments of golden light twinkles when thinking about how Eve looked. She will likely appear more face-to-face now. She has a white halo, but it's filmy. That's a good thing still. She hangs her head slightly with closed eyelids. The Holy Spirit remarks, saying, "She is pleased you would take notice." One small white flower with five petals and a gold center was offered from the very spirited lady. "I am Eve, don't fret over saying who I am," she brings to us with her special wording appearing, and still very much through vocalization.

Anything that the Lord wants revealed is fine with the interpreter. "You wonder about the power instilled inside of Father God's soul," Jesus speaks out on. People think the spirit is an unusual manifestation. "We wonder, God. We wonder, Jesus," prayer was necessary. "He is a power to be reckoned with still," the words which appeared. The interpreter is still sitting here waiting for the Lord to let us in on God's other secrets about His own creations. He has a slew of ideas, but sometimes being patient for the answer we need will have to do. "I am Father God, Maker of heaven and earth and all mankind," He's sending. He says, "Tell them He visits everyone." God was speaking for Himself too. God makes you wonder if He spun around in swift moving circles or something to create Himself. "I didn't do that but I know what you want to hear," Father God sent with dark lettered words to appear before the interpreter's very own eyes. The closeness is real, and mostly unusual.

Blue-white light flashed near the floor. Kind of neat to see resembling very cold ice in a way, but the Holy Spirit is still very kind, not a heavenly Father and Savior who would make you agonize. A super sized black garden tool favoring a spade sets inside of orange light. A white light which glows like sunshine has covered the spade now. Why? The interpreter doesn't know why until the Lord specifies what His purpose was for sharing this spiritual vision when visiting Him. Orange sunlight from inside of heaven, aside the white light with soft rays, now it sheds warm sun between the roots inside of a small mound of dirt which is being held onto.

Do we really need warm sunlight to reach roots in the ground? "We believe it helps," the Holy Spirit responded. A woman with gardener gloves on holds a potted flower into the air. She is on her knees. Her dark scarf is creased down the middle. Now the base of the plant is covered in gold foil. "I planted flowers on earth, but they are easy to manage here," she said. It is possible to get her name, but even the interpreter knows that takes some doing. The name "Kathy" appeared. That was easier than thought to be. From past experiences names have come easily from the spirit world, but you'll find when relaxing with prayer and meditation the Lord will show them when you let Him do His work without pushing Him. Too many times we want what we want when we want it in a big rush. Her lily flower wrapped in foil had a serene red dash of light touching the upper and outside edges of the plant's petals.

It is finally Easter. Aglow is the Lord's youthful face from the beam off the side and bottom of a yellow candle. It has a pointed white flame, and that wasn't where most of the iridescence effect came from when upon the Lord's face now. "I am the Savior you have come to know," Jesus is talking in the spirit on this very special day. Every day should be looked upon as exceptional, besides such a great time of the year as this. What will Jesus add in about rising from the grave? "What will you add Jesus?" asked in prayer. "My thoughts are sincere and good," He sends back. He will begin again. "The resurrection helped me understand your feelings too," Jesus knows what He is talking about, whether you believe the interpreter or not. Yes we are entitled to our freedom in heaven, and by the feeling we have of the Lord, He'll continue doing the very best for us. Not one but two white pillows are pressed against the Lord's head. Does He have a place of rest for us? "The comfort you will receive will be immeasurable," He declared. These messages are all up to every split-second that they were received and rendered.

Some kids are bouncing around inside of the spirit world dressed like bunny rabbits. Kids in the light always get your attention. It is Easter and these rosy red cheek children have little treats to eat and even lightweight baskets. A little brown haired girl with chocolate color eyes is one of the many children bending over to thoroughly enjoy what looks like an egg rolling contest. Okay, now the interpreter gets her. She is having fun with white eggs too. Not to say she doesn't have any colorful eggs, she probably does somewhere. The smaller amount to the oval eggs were pointing upward over her eyebrows, while she was covering both eyes. The eggs lowered slowly to where her very brown eyes came into view again. A slow but interesting move seen before in the light. She has very soft shades of golden light upon her face. "Children really find Easter fascinating here in heaven," are words shown in black lettering.

With a couple of shiny gold horseshoes surfacing inside of the light, one is upside down compared to the upright shoe. The Lord feels that if you use His knowledge of signs and wonders by testing them out for a questioning and answering session to your vantage point, using such a vision through prayer in meditation will help to determine a final outcome to questions. Put a little simpler perhaps. In prayer the interpreter will ask the Lord for the answer to an important question he has. Our Lord will also be asked to show either an upright horseshoe or the one that's pointing downward, for the yes or no answer to be returned. "Testing the spirit is not a sin," Jesus just spoke inside of the Holy Spirit. You see, Jesus wants you to prosper.

More than one python are rearing their ugly heads. Naturally the Lord appreciates seeing His heavenly Father's creatures which are the shown examples of them. Now one about five feet high appears inside of the interpreter's work area. The tongue is out and it's a little too much. The Lord coming around with these creatures again is unusual. A pterodactyl grabbed the python by the neck. It's spiritual, but quite yucky, though the Lord has His reasons. Funny, the pterodactyl is completely yellow in color. "There were creatures unknown to everyone, but you'll have knowledge later," the Holy Spirit sends in a message. That's nice to know scientists don't everything. You'll really enjoy what the Lord is doing now.

A very ornate golden lamp appears with a small upturn handle. It would remind you of a gravy boat, or even a genie's magical lamp. Words appeared in the spirit which read: Make a wish. If you believe in miracles they will happen. The lamp expands now much wider. A smoky gold stream of light is floating above the spout of sorts. You know who the interpreter is looking for? A genie! God has all power, and that's true, but He and the Lord have miracle workers in the light as well. Golden light begins to glow from someone's winding white turban. The genie has a gold mustache and beard. He has folded prayer hands with a small golden cross sitting upright upon them. We can benefit from making wishes while we are in prayer with the Lord, and whoever we shall choose to believe in as holy and wise, such as Father God and the very lovely Virgin Mary, it is all good.

"Try to be peaceful while on earth," an Indian in the coolest caramel-vanilla shade of holy light says. How can one be sure he is an Indian visiting? There was a straight feather upon his head, and as he now positioned himself on a couple of angles quickly. The Indian's hands remain open with his baby fingers matched up and glowing with radiating gold light.

"We are very visual for you, the reason is to be helpful to people," Jesus related. Predictions of the future can vary due to some of the tragedies being avoidable. The Holy Spirit advises, "Use your forethought." When you feel there is a warning inside listen to your feelings closely. Better to be more aware of your surroundings then. The other side feels tragedies can be avoided no matter how big they have been or may become. "Certain people have the ability to foresee the future," the Lord sends to us with a comfortable expression. The Holy Spirit actually just said, "The interpreter doesn't know everything." And you just know that wouldn't flow from the interpreter's mouth so freely unless he was guided to say such a thing about himself. That's sort of a relief, because there are some who will wonder why disasters in the past weren't reported. The afterlife even believes there are problems with some predictions being explained, too.

How can we spend so much time with the Lord before death? The same way we can after death. Spiritual people tend to have a more developed mind. More kindness and understanding. A happy man is saying, when rubbing his left wrist around a little, "A gold watch was given to me." It's a real beauty. "The smile is from living here with the Lord," he says, while it's obvious he was reading someone's thoughts on our side. "The way I can be seen is from prayer only," he now states clearly, but that would be for others. Is he super important? He is, but as important as our very own on his side of life. Inside of the heavens he is happy as well. That smile won't leave his face, and he doesn't have to even try hard to keep it. He claims, "I am a scholar of yours." Maybe he is a metaphysician too. "Please accept me as a friend," he included in his messaging, while a massive orange soothing light is comfortable for him to feel. "Your brain waves should coincide with the Holy Spirit," he was quick to point out. So we shall pray to Jesus when prayer is needed. The theory is that we find peace and love inside of the spirit. Yellow bird has returned standing above an open Bible created with glorious layers of fine gold. That Bible is an amazing sight, and so is the little birdie.

Can you for a minute picture the little one gazing at the inside pages? Very funny, and a calmness has set in. Can birds read? "Not exactly difficult for them to understand words," told from the heavenly realm, after asking in a private prayer to the Lord. Parrots have a knack of picking up words too. If Jesus feel birds have certain abilities then so be it. "They are genius, my friend," Jesus shares. A pale blue arching light appeared over the interpreter's left knee. "It is inside as well," the Holy Spirit concluded. Funny how the shape was overlapping.

"You would be surprised if you knew who they were who just came to visit," a version of words seen. Not Father God, but friends of His. "I am not Father God like you first had thought," he is saying. Soft white beards, straight hair down to their shoulders and velvety smooth mustaches are trending in the heavens. "I will guide you for now," one comes speaking as a servant for our Father God. He holds a thin brown wood cross close to his face on his right cheek as he feels love for it and for Christ. The cross presses against the center of his face now, to where he can see on each side of the middle stick of wood. A perfect mask in a way, so Christlike in his appearance, he is one with Christ and His Maker. Mint green eternal light glows upon his face in an "x" shape spread out evenly and very softly. A pink and orange band of light is approaching without any strings attached to them, and as the eternal rays come they have the appearance of gliders in the air. Before they were seen as a pink strip of light over the orange, but now each width of color exists very close to the Lord's cupped hands. Like arrows without sharp ends they are part of His plan.

Always feel encouraged to carry on in life, that's the way God and His Son want it to be. Can gold sparkle inside of a straight line of darkness? It just did and that's what was so uncanny. What a beautiful sight from God. The Lord says, "Many people have prayed in war camps." We have a conveyer it appears as a woman on her knees. She is able to send us a message from heaven. "I'm really a special person. Feel the same," she says. How is it so that someone would from the other side of life, a place commonly known as heaven, could come here inside of the Holy Spirit and speak to us about her once being held beyond her will? This woman, by her own example of what she went through shows us she's wearing a very thin garment, that of a dress which was so tattered and faded. "That was all I had. You shouldn't feel that it's wrong to respond," she was saying.

From the sight of her hands held out a morsel of food was all she was fed. "You would be right about that. I knew we would be free someday," she said. Again, visible words appear from heaven. "See my pretty flower the Lord has given me? I enjoy yellow flowers," she said. But, she and her friends also prayed for food to come. "We scarcely had enough to stay alive," our chestnut brown haired lady said. Somehow she instantly changed into a white gown given to her from the Lord. She has a white carnation above her heart. You'd like it if you saw it on her. "Try to speak truthfully," she says. More or less she is very instrumental with us communicating with the other side. She doesn't feel your interpreter is being dishonest, she is being very polite. "We could hardly believe the war ended. I spent a long time recuperating before I felt good inside," she said. She shows a full loaf of uncovered bread and felt that it was a real feast for her. Her hands are buried in her face. Unfortunately she felt really bad. But, she wants you to know she has a smile on her face during this period of her life. "I can wear what I want in heaven. Believe you me, you will enjoy heaven," she ended with because she must go. She thoroughly enjoyed talking with us. A person the interpreter wants to spend more life experiences with in the future, that is, over on her side when the time comes. She could talk.

"Don't worry so much about the communications we have. I'll provide you with plenty of knowledge," Jesus says as He looks very proud. The Lord will reveal your own shortcomings back to you. Maybe in a vision or perhaps He will mention something about them inside of a dream for you to learn from. "If you could only feel compassion. Think of me as your friend guiding you daily," the Lord mentions. He has the right to say what He did, He's not accusing anyone of having less compassion for people. Negative feelings such as anger and rebellion have taken a beating. But from what we have heard lately from a woman who was once inside of a war camp and had survived, we were very compassionate with her, a helpful lesson to understand that deep feeling we have inside for people as we felt quite a bit of peace within her presence. She knew what you were thinking before, and probably a little bit more after from her departure.

A small shed very old looking with a slanted roof is not without orange and white shades of light from the "holy" upon it. You'd naturally think God was telling us that if someone were visiting the inside to work, or to maybe retrieve work tools, and there was sudden death befallen upon oneself, the Lord's protective light would be there to lift you up. "Thank you for helping me describe the light. Many people have died in unusual places," Jesus sends in a verbalized message now. Not so weak of a sign and message after all.

A woman draped in a dark towel is grasping the side of a her bathtub. She did plead for help because of an ailing heart. "I knew help was coming," she says. The left side of her face is creased by a mild golden and white light as she looks upward into heaven. "The love is overwhelming here," she describes her place of well-being. She slumped over her tub, and she became an overwhelmingly big presence inside of the Holy Spirit as she witnessed her own death. It wasn't an ugly sight to see herself down below wrapped in her towel. "I knew I would be taken care of," she explains in all sincerity. The Lord relieved her from the pain of dying.

Pink vibrations of eternal light are very distinctive especially when becoming softer like that because of the lightness in tone extending more into the heavens now. A mysterious object appears in gold, rounded with a black emblem in the middle with a white ball of light. A small gold arrow points to the pink light, and it brightens. Mid-air supernatural activity occurs. The spirit moves in closer for your comfort. A small row of red roses with nice green leaves are growing in front of a brown log. There isn't anything dirty about that. A boy and girl stand at each end of the row of flowers, and white water sprinkles out from their cans. A white beam of light up above the children is the size of a giant mushroom top. "We peek at you too," the children say. They need to see us. Look for the brown log. White figures in the holy light will come. Now they have a golden light around them too. You may have seen them in heaven this way before anyone else. Even before they were described within the light the second time around.

Funny but an ivory "Queen" piece was a spiritual sight. "Our Virgin Mary is our Queen too," we have sent to you in a message. Her left foot is visible, and blue light glows upon Her toes. Her white robe spreading in style near heaven's floor in the spirit is pure and elegant. "Thank you for looking at my robe in the spirit," Mary says. She really had to help with the words then. She even said, "That's good." Both feet are now very visible and She would have you know they are resting upon a billowy type of cloud. Also very scalloped around the edges it's quite a beautiful rest stool. Ivory arms to Her throne appear. How very vivid of a vision. Now it is not hart saying why She said what She did. "My throne is quite a nice place to be seated," She tries to explain. A small amount of white comes in next and a word next to the opening. Then more words come through for us from Her. "My heart is with you is why. I appreciate them knowing how I feel is why," She tells everyone. Mary thought someone was a little funny the way he was acting. She may also wonder about some of the females as well. "The children of heaven have special activities with me," our Savior's Mother said, while many small infants remain inside of Her arms. "I feel like a Queen, my friends," believe it or not our Queenly Mother Mary announces this from Her throne.

While experiencing a little nerve ending pain, the Holy Spirit sends a message about that. He would have people experiencing the same feeling of discomfort, to try relaxing inside of your mind. Some of the ailments come from the way we think. "You feel more at ease now," the Holy Spirit relates in words appearing, and they are right too. Your interpreter feels much calmer after a pausing, sitting straight as possible with all thought basically escaping one's own thought patterns. The peace was extraordinary and the nerve pain went away, likely due to the Lord's powerful suggestion He secretly sent through, with more conveyance to others, firsthand. The Lord is right, but you'll feel He puts you in the right perspective when acquiring that great peace of mind when we accept His guidance in our life. If He says to relax in your mind, indulge without haste. All of the "He said," and

"She said" speech patterns from the heavens can be fully agreed upon as, 'Immediate Messages Sent from Heaven.'

"Let your mind be filled with pleasant thoughts," comes from the Holy Spirit. If there was ever a friendly ghost in your house it would be Jesus in the spirit. He will tell you what's right if you care to listen. A dark green strip of light appears. Kind of odd? It seems so because of the dirty looking color to the specter. Still, God and the Lord must be respected for every which way they help us. Maybe an odder vision to help us appreciate the colorful visitations and open aspects of heaven more. The Holy Spirit moved across the room in ten intervals. The split-second intervals, as brief as they were really meant something. Two large hands held high and a table of stone covered with sunlight shining upon it was a clue as to why the number ten seems so important. Heaven really does have a thing about the ten commandments. + The cross was accidentally hit on the interpreter's keyboard, but it so important to everybody that we will just let it remain without disturbing the holy symbol.

"Thank you for the flowers, Jesus," expresses the interpreter. Red roses from the Lord should help you cheer up. A spirit of a child or an adult is playing with a huge ball of kite string. The string is being wound back into an arch, but the spiritual human hasn't appeared, only a spooky demonstration, pertaining to bizarre activity inside of the spirit. A boy thinks the interpreter knows who he is, but he's keeping "mum." "Is that right, Lord?" asked of the Lord "He is visiting you," Jesus responds. The boy wound up all of the string from the ball all around a white stick of light. A yellow kite flies around inside of heaven and has enough wind to even take on a new direction of its own as it turns. "Kids enjoy kite flying," a spiritual sign, which includes words in such a speech pattern to understand. Have you ever seen a kite fly in heaven? You will once you are here in heaven. Doesn't it sound weird to hear such words from your interpreter? He is in heaven with these wonderful events going on because of the six sense becoming far-advanced. The little boy reeled in his kite quite quickly. The skies of heaven are filled with almost every color a kite can be, especially in what the Lord would call inside "picnic areas." Festive events continue daily.

Time to watch the Holy Spirit of the Lord. Where is the Lord? A silent thought. For all others, ask yourself the same question and lift your eyes up inside of the spirit world. Where is that located? Right there in your kitchen, your bedroom, or even on your patio outside. Open your beautiful eyes up more and more. The Lord is coming to you. It shouldn't take more than five minutes to see the Lord, and you'd be amazed to know that Jesus exhibited that amount of time with a small clock and the numeral. About half that amount of time has passed by with the interpreter waiting on the Lord to appear. Since He is here, the Lord may as well commence revealing the shape of Himself now. Jesus comes through, especially with the shoulder length hair, but what has never been seen before in this manner was a shiny black robe in front of the white garment He wears. It doesn't completely cover His own robe, but it was held up in comparison to the one He has on. The outer edge was where you can see the white one presently.

There was a white carnation attached to the black robe, and it's possible it's the robe He has chosen for you upon your arrival. Hold on we will find out why. "My children are awarded beautiful robes is why. God is expecting you in the future," the Lord quickly responds when being sought after in the light. We will think that it's a big relief to be with our Father.

Some habits are good to have. The Lord can suddenly move about in the spirit to get your attention when need be, especially when you should be aware of what is coming. An image of a speeding car in miniature form whipped on by in the light, and sure enough one went by while glancing out the livingroom window. The Lord has a habit of waking up our senses. "Center your thoughts into the light," Jesus suggests.

A gentleman sitting in heaven is very amused by flourishing orange light that is stretching back inside of the heavens with people pointing into it with overwhelming thoughts and feelings about the wonderful sight. Even so two early regions of white light points outward into many directions mostly around him and the people. "I suggest you draw in the orange light around you. Picture it moving in close to each side of your body," the gentleman speaks of. Does the light crisscross within our inner being and soul after that or what? "Concentrate on it taking control a little bit. Don't let it bother you what is said," the person of interest sitting in the chair relayed. You can meditate that way if you like.

An owl seemed to be peering into a white crystal ball, but after clearing the mind from that thought, it was perceived that he was concentrating on the holy light inside heaven. The Lord is here. He said, "I am surprised that you learned that from me." How very thoughtful of the Lord. Not only is He surprised, we all are.

And that sudden deep yearning for our family, out of the blue, how we long to be with our loved ones who have been long gone for some time now. Let's see what Jesus would like to say to you again about your family. Asked in prayer, "Lord, what would you say to your own people to help them feel more comfortable about their family?" He knows the question is about people in heaven. "My dear loved ones, do not fret. Let the Lord reveal to you who they are," He said. Jesus also agrees with what was said. "Recognizing them in the light will be easy. You should let the Lord bring them out into the open," the Lord recommends. While looking upward toward heaven Jesus appears with three lambs, one in His arms and two in front of Him. He's not trying to humiliate you, but He can make many wishes come true. Someone is tugging at their right ear. The Holy Spirit wants you to imagine at first, your family is coming through the light like that. Then it will happen. You'll know best who you'll want coming. Unbelievable!

"I'm doing fine," the interpreter's mother said, using words. There she was during a little intense concentration searching her out, when picturing her tugging on her ear she came through like magic. A very soft white robe, and her dark hair is really nice looking. But it's all about you and the Lord. Come on now, stretch your eyes a little bit and look upward into the light. Someone close is about to tug at your heart strings.

Our Lord's majestic gold crown is huge on display with wording describing what the Lord is all about and what happened when He arrived in heaven. Across the front of His crown read: Crowned. That word appeared in black lettering. "I am pleased you took notice," exactly how the Lord talks and feels. He feels it takes time for the interpreter to discern. A black candle has spiking white light inside the circle where a wick must be located. It hasn't been spotted yet. The rounded ball of light is so spectacular. "My thoughts are similar," the Lord just communicated.

The Lord's pretty yellow tulips make not one, but two angel wings somehow. They arch like backward halves to heart shapes. Above there is a small halo made from three yellow tulips, the same number used for the Lord's wings He just created. "Pray for answers," the Lord instructed now. A child in a soft white robe glides in close to the interpreter, and he's wearing the small tulips, those which have made superb wings for flight and a gorgeous halo to be enjoyed. The blend was unusual but pretty. "Don't worry about my name," he says. Funny how those five words came in clearly, but when it came to finding his name it was more of a struggle. That's from trying to hard to impress. Let the children lead the way. It is very nice to be visiting heaven today. "Im trying to tell you something special to hear. You will become holier than you are now," he said and what a relief that is, the acceptance of the Holy Spirit's grace and divine intervention. The boy's floating on air with a white ruffled angel in front of him, that one which is so fluffed up, that his large size angelical wing friend would remind you of a floating swan.

A short break brought the interpreter of spiritual messages even closer inside of the Lord's arms more so. While taking a short walk a light blue candle lay flat on the floor, and while wondering how to avoid it, not to step on the holy image, it was decided upon to keeping walking forward. Not only did it remain visible a foot away, but it became possible to walk over the candle with it passing through one's legs. It was completely level against the flooring which was so unique. Keep on walking into the light, and if you happen to look back to earth one day while doing so, you'll be feeling very comfortable thinking about your loved ones you've left behind. It is because of the peace of mind God gives you. You'll still feel concerned over everyone and it will show on your face. "I can help you overcome sadness my friends. My Father is special to love," our most cordial King explains. His Father will be merciful, don't worry about the wrongs.

A long white canoe is bouncing up and down on top of flowing water. So far no accidents. One man is rowing and he is also inside of the heavens. Known due to a white tunnel of light in front of him, but he's still finds it to be a task to maneuver his canoe. "Im a boat enthusiast. I have a few boats here in heaven," he says. If he says so. He feels a lot of people are enthused about the spirit world. "The rivers are very interesting. You shouldn't worry about dying, I too felt the same way as you," he adds in the conversation. Jesus appears clearly and says, "You should keep learning about our side of life." "The Lord has many boats in heaven. You will alarm many people by what has been already said," our canoe lover states.

The tinier white bell flower with a sparkly gold chip of light in the center has in fact decorated the Lord's face and hair. Many of the flowers cover His hair and beard, which was first noticed. Zooming in on His nose a small one gently rests upon the top of it. He is twirling one around in front of His face, close enough to draw attention to His eyes. They are still very beautiful and blue, but you can't even see them during this moment. Why? Because the Lord's eyes are filled with the tiny bell flowers. Actually one flower covering each eye. "I am the creative type too," He speaks of in a very mannerly way. A gold cross appears on top of a distant mountain. What looks like vapors coming out from the Lord's mouth in a white spray of light was Him breathing life into the cross. The cross glows brightly when all is said and done.

Do you think that maybe the Lord shouldn't be talking the way He does in this transcription, and the interpreter should just go away somewhere and be quiet? Don't feel that way, the Lord has many surprises for you that are coming up very soon. A black ship's wheel appeared, a reminder that the Lord, the Virgin Mary and our heaven Father God are still our guides, but when it comes to managing our lives we must be in full control of the ship.

An invisible hand which became visible, if you can understand that talk, has been printing something in black letters across a stretched out parchment of paper. If you think seeing a hand write without an arm attached is strange you haven't seen anything yet. The hand is holding a white feathery pin that's moving across the paper with a little bit of hesitation too. That has to be studied. It read: Remember we will always love you. The Holy Spirit interjected, "You should explain the message thoroughly." So there must be more to be read across the parchment given unto us. Another message read: Please don't worry about what you are feeling. There's a decent amount of innocence that settles in your emotions when you feel God has selected you to carry His message for Him. A glistening gold string was tied into a small bow to hold the roll of paper together now. The one hand wasn't visible this time it just ended up tied. The Lord mentions, "Across the globe families mourn the loss of their loved ones today." Three people are here inside of the Holy Spirit. They cup their hands close to their faces as they have been stricken with grief. An upside down solid triangle of golden light in that formation attaches itself to their hands and points downward, although a beautiful sight of light upon them, they're still deeply disturbed over the passing of people close to them. "They've come into the light. They were crying, relieving themselves of sorrow," the Lord just said.

"I'll tell you what to say," a woman of around thirty years of age says. She begins again. "People are restored to youth and should come as no surprise," she speaks of. She thinks heaven is a marvelous place like the rest of us do. She does have waves of shoulder length golden blonde hair. She is gorgeous. She giggles almost as if she was tickled pink. Her hands curl in front of her midriff area as she is mostly covered in white light while wearing a long gown. As she stands inside of the Holy Spirit with such a wonderful gladness about her splendid life in heaven, her upper chest forms a white heart from the inner squeezing of herself. You are probably correct to believe her breasts formed the heart against her white robe. Golden light sparkles and swirls above her head to form a perfect halo ring, that which also leaves a trail of the glitter. Soft gold light before her suggests, not only is she watching what is inside, she was a very fast learner of how delightful it was to be surrounded by her Lord's grandness of the heavens.

A flash camera comes in unexpectedly. "It makes you feel like a star," the Lord insists. Without really thinking so at first, the idea of being involved with the Lord in heaven will make us feel that way. Huge lights used on movies sets are elevating in white light, and perhaps it's a secret message for someone who's involved with acting. God knows the spiritual interpreter doesn't have the time or effort to be involved with the silver screen. There is someone listening who will have a chance at that. If the Lord brings us a glowing gold ladybug you're going to hear about it. He did make one enter the physical plane.

Not to sound selfish and to be bragging about the other side so much, but you should hear about the out of body experience the interpreter experienced in his sleep. It has been spoken of in the past, how you'll have the chance to pray to go up and away on a pleasant journey on the special spiritual fulfilling amusement ride in the heavens. That would be on 'The Whirling White Light Ride in Heaven.' After being fast asleep for several hours the Holy Spirit intervened inside the vast clear heavens above, placing the interpreter inside a deep scalloped white cloud, not exactly hollowed out, but one might say "deep dished." You become seated inside when you go on that ride, where you'll clearly see many rays of soft white light spreading up and above you. When you start moving forward it will be to ascend the majestic heavens. And golden light will be surrounding you and the ride. Mostly what is most memorable is the love of God that you'll feel. What the Lord has to say about the ride now. "You're an experienced diviner when it comes to describing the ride you are talking about," Jesus speaks of while showing words to convey His message. Many will enjoy this magnificent ride. It will come to many as a big surprise, especially for those who've sought it out.

Blue violets swirl in heaven. The Lord is smelling a white carnation inside orange light. Two more white carnations rest near His feet as He stands bending over just a little. It was strange to hear from the Lord, "Too many instances of angels will bother a few people." That is very unfortunate for the very few who are not interested in hearing about their existence. Perhaps that sounds harsh to some, but hopefully we will all be getting along through the rest of these privileged messages coming from heaven.

People in the light are talking about how much their puffy black hats are admired. Maybe a bit fuzzy, but they are really soft. Fixed in the back and touched lightly in front to one for this lucky person in heaven to be styled with. A thin white cross on His chest positioned upon his black silk robe. Also someone wearing a white carnation too. "Many of us enjoy living in style here. Let the spirit move you," the visiting manly spirit of a fellow said. A woman wearing long golden earrings has the same styled hat upon her head. "I love you," from inside of the very Holy Spirit. A tall gold cross glows with edges of white light upon it. A golden Roman number two appeared with a blue swath of light for the base. A gold swath of light across the top. They become large with curving inner structure forming columns. A small dove descends from the heavens within gold light. The light vanished temporarily, and the dove is pearly white with gold spots, and that's a mystery. Unless you are in heaven understanding their disposition.

A bent stemmed white rose ascends up into heaven. A black telephone receiver appears with a white pointer nearly touching the mouthpiece. "We want people to hear the message," Jesus conveyed. Play some music while digesting the transcript, you will feel a lot better. "Your faith is most honorable," Jesus related to the interpreter after receiving a message about prayer for a sick person. The Holy Spirit wishes for a brief interval for receiving interesting spiritual messages coming from a world beyond to our very own.

"It loosens up your mind to sing," Jesus begins saying in His holy vibrations of movement and precious words. You know He's right about that. Wow does it ever feel good to sing. Jesus seemed to be tucking in a huge white angle beneath Himself, but no, He was actually letting it be free out in the open of others. He can handle His angels very well. A small child's school desk comes through the white light very much grounded. "We will be teaching you lessons in life.

Be ready to learn," Jesus and God is instructing. The genius will be instilled for learning still. On either side of life. Many presents inside of various white boxes with black bows will be presented when people arrive in heaven, especially to make us happier. There will also be various gift wrapped packages. It was told too. Two round gold balls of glistening light are decorations sitting upon silky black folds of cloth in heaven. The gifts are together with them near.

We realize that God and the Lord along with our Virgin Mary, within our presence, will be enough of a wonderful gift when they greet us in life after death. The Lord didn't have to show us more gifts, but He did any ways. How rich can our Lord really be to be ever so remindful of Him caring that much? White light flashes. "We are glad you are on our team," the messaging just came from a Lord known as Jesus Christ, the One who is as tall as your ceiling. His white robe is huge! The ceiling in here is pretty high. His garment swept behind Him, and it's actually easy on the eyes and so very soft and pleasing to see. "I'm able to visit everyone. Just be receptive and I'll visit you now," are the Lord's exact words. A sliver light flashes upon the interpreter's dark shirt. The color of silver is so peaceful when it comes from the Lord directing it to shine.

A small black and gold ribbon are joined. They would be given out at pie contests or inside of the Holy Spirit for the fun of it. A long flat box is wrapped with dark paper and a big black bow. Twinkly gold falls upon the gift and a person in the light begins tugging at the loose end to unwrap the package. The lid lifts up. Golden peaks of light reach the top of the box. Similar to a pinnacle. A beam of gold light from beyond touches down inside of the box and raises a crown upward from the inside. Hands turn the crown around where a ball of white light on the front begins glowing. Two wide white candles of perfection were resulted from the crown's radiation.

A tall Shepherd's cane is set pretty close to the Lord's chest and He looks over us still. Surprised is the best way to describe the way He stands inside of the spirit world and right here this minute where we live. Even more surprisingly, the Lord's eyes are adjust so evenly that He sees on each side of the cane near the curve with an equal amount of eyesight used. Very good thinking. "If you focus you will understand," the Lord instructs. Even if you think there's something wrong with your health and it bothers you to go see a doctor, you should go any ways. "We are rooting behind the scenes for you," the spirit of the Lord sends in a message.

A black man sitting upon an ivory throne himself is quite a presence. He has some green light covering a small but notable portion on the upper part of his face. He is very big in stature. As he sits upon the high seat His image begins changing to where He looked like the Lord sitting in the dark. The long hair and all, but His facial features became solid black. "My son you have knowledge of Father God in heaven. Bring my people closer to me in conversation," either God or the Lord announces. The spiritual presence has a different image which has already become known to the interpreter. His face becomes so snowy white and His hair is still shoulder length identical to Jesus. Outlines to unusual forms move from left to right, more than once or twice. Time to capture the full image. Jesus is here. "I will tell you something, you love people with all of your heart," He spoke using visible wording to help us along. Have a nice day. You can see Him too, you know better to ignore Him when He comes through with wisdom provided on how to visualize Him. "Count to three and you will see an arching white angel where I stand," said instantly with the Holy Spirit guiding you now.

Distinct markings in the spirit. "It pains me to listen," a voice of the spirit world is saying. The person speaking is white robed, bending way over almost down on her or his knees with hands covering both ears. This much is true. Not expected from the heavens? Best to be acquainted with the help. "It's transparent is why," the person relates about golden light crystals, those which shine in a tall cross. Who is that? Unbelievable to hear this about the funny person up there. It is a "he." Facial expressions are very suggestive, and so are his upturned hands close to his face. "I am a playful guide," he suddenly relates using letters from the alphabet for readable words in the light. Perhaps he can hear the prayers sent up to the Lord and for God. And, to all other important saints. "I hear prayers made to the Lord," whom he only mentions. That's all good to hear from him in heaven. He's important but apparently he has heard much all at once.

The dark curly haired man holds a black Bible in his right hand near his hip, how you'd carry your school books home. Bible is spelled in gold letters on the spine of the book. Likely on the front as well, but for now, that came in exceptionally well. What can't he stand hearing over there? He must know so many things in heaven that would last for an eternity. What doesn't he know when shrugging his shoulders? Something else he did. He'll have to be asked these questions in prayer, through the Holy Spirit naturally. "It pains me to hear nonsense from your side," he refers to. A tall microphone on a stand was just seen with him probably being responsible for bringing it here. It's an "open microphone" with them up above. "A distance away conversations are heard from where you live. My goal is to provide you with information," the guide mentioned. A thin black "V" he is illustrating with little balls of white glowing light upon the top. It stood for "Victory." The word appeared capitalized in the splendid vision.

A pink flower is very fresh, and the vibrant green grass beneath it is unearthly. Speakers often convey necessary messages, sitting up high behind half-circled white rings of light, where they're important people acting in our behalf. They look like councilmen and women. "There will be a lot of messages about your stay in heaven," it was conveyed. Don't be alarmed by the message. One of the women in the spiritual setting leans over the top of the fancy glowing tabletop to draw our attention to the white cross with a silver gild.

It only takes a split second to arrive in heaven, inevitably from a massive heart attack taking place. You'll feel comfort in knowing it's not the end of the world, only the beginning of a new life for everyone. Faith in God and the Lord will carry you to heaven, it will show in the courage you have during what seems like the very end. "I'll be with you at the end of your life," the Lord insures as He speaks. You can believe that the Lord is really sending you these messages, all which are up to the minute, as you see, the interpreter has nothing to lose, one who has much faith in Jesus. Even after one heart attack, severe pain in the heart region has been such a hinder lately that it seemed like any moment the curtains would be closing on this side for him. But wait just a minute, there is still enough hope left to believe in better dieting with a healthier lifestyle to come. We shall see what the Lord will say about that in just a minute.

A real banana and a gold pear becomes visible inside of the Holy Spirit, so no nonsense about what the Lord reveals as being good for what ails you, besides what we should be eating on an ongoing basis. "People in the South Seas have the right idea about eating," a message about them from the other side. The most beautiful baby blue light eases in from heaven, whereas it widens more on this side, but extends greatly far into the next life. Quite a walkway. The Lord suggested that more of His blueness be drawn in through the top of our head, thinking about how wonderful it would be as our own halo as well. That's what He shows a baby blue ring of a halo that sheds light throughout our entire self.

Baby blue wings, a gold aura with an endless shine, a giggling soulful spirit embodied of it becomes transparent as the angel slides through the back of the blue pathway and now across the front as though sliding on ice."I am an angel," was said as one golden sparkle shines.

A small fish about four inches long hangs on a fisherman's hook, but suddenly a large gold fish hangs from the line. A white Persian cat is licking her chops, and that comes from the other side. The fish swirls off the line now. "Don't use grease in cooking," seemed to be the words seen. The cat looked hungry. A message about not indulging in the wrong way of preparing it supposedly. Three huge bowls of green lettuce and a magical person in the light is trying to relate more to us about nourishment. Hands were tossing salad around and around. There is a person visiting. "It actually was what you thought," was said about the vision of all of the lettuce turning into huge heads of cauliflower. That was nice of our helper clarifying it before the interpreter goes bananas. Going from lettuce to cauliflower was a neat trick.

The interpreter had to chuckle, but now it's uncertain of if he should have. It seems his home is open to everyone in heaven who wanted to visit. A person wearing whale teeth on a dipping necklace finds it comfortable to stand in the corner. The spirit has to be of a man because his chest is bare without real bosoms like a woman has. He has a very dark chest. So far no head. He winces because he knows what was said about him, wherefore he appeared more out into the open. He is funny. He comes back to cauliflower with a huge hunk being nibbled. Very much handheld which is surprising to see him exhibiting and consuming food too. "My ways will enlighten you," he said. Very handsome is he. So brown with a beard and mustache and hair to wish for if you were a balding man. He raises higher in the spirit world, not touching the floor anymore where the interpreter lives. "You should pay heed to the warnings you receive," he says, as heavenly swirls of white figures with golden balls of light keep changing in shape. The kind of creations that stop you in your tracks and make you want to say, "heaven."

A large outline of an angel, a small white ball of light and a huge shading of blue, which comes to shelter us from damnation. Just an educated guess of to why the Lord is doing what He feels He ought to. "I"ll allow that to be said," Jesus announces unexpectedly. The Lord feels the interpreter is a little sad about the slow down right now. Where does this slow motion feeling inside come from any ways? Praise the Lord for energy and hopefully more will come about. The Holy Spirit is here showing dozens of important things, and now is the time for all good men to go to work again. After it was brought to the interpreter's attention to draw white light in from behind it was experimented with. The brain seemed to unknot some which is always a sign of relief to come. "Stretch a little that will help," a spiritual message arrived. It feels like morning when we wake up and stretch out our arms. Everything feels better after stretching and releasing.

When old friends visit in the spirit you really know how lucky you are to be appreciated. An older black man who has been a friend for many long years died and went to heaven. Today he visits while slowly turning the brim to his favorite hat around. That's how your's truly could tell who just came in through a mild orange holy light. The interpreter is Caucasian and that's what makes it so special, all nationalities being able to see eye to eye. He is a fine man who can make you feel young again just by hearing him talking nicely. Maybe a special gift instilled, he has it all, especially where he is right now. He's here in the Holy Spirit as well, so why don't we find out what has to say. He looks a lot younger. "I had a feeling you would seek me out in the light," he says. He's very jovial in heaven, very much told and felt by the way he excels back in through aspects of gold swaths of light.

A wiggling worm moves about freely, then it stops in front of an open book. Very funny to see as though cartoons were on. "We know you dislike insects," the spirit world says. Although that may be true with many of us, in heaven they can be very funny acting. Specs of yellow have formed a thick halo over the worm. No kidding just part of nature in another land. The insect life is more unusual. We'll study insects in heaven. While wondering about the cures they bring from serious illness the answer given back was, "Not too many cures." But there was more of a sign given about studying flowers more. "You think there's an answer to cure cancer," Jesus speaks about from the spirit world. "Well is there, Lord?" the interpreter asked in prayer. "Use prayer to help with your cancer," Jesus sent to you and me in guiding our future better.

Another scroll unwinds. It is very white with some sort of golden design on each end which the paper rolls from. On the front our message read: Peace my friends. Lucid light moves softly. Some things can be hard to explain perfectly. Colorful birds appear everywhere, and they're also duplicate images of the same creature, but in all white. A sparrow stands behind an open hymn book. The word "tweet" appeared in small black letters. That was really something else besides just cute. "Our mystical Father will excite you with many wonders," the message, but you decide if it's true. The start of your life is with the Lord. "I am able to give you things but you must grow first," Jesus said now. The interpreter wants to see Him today and is having a hard time seeing His face. Usually it doesn't take long, so this is a first.

His white sleeve appears with Him holding the Bible in His hand. A very nice gold cross glows upon the cover. "You should know I am here," He spells out in words. There are very thick vanilla clouds in heaven. A favorite sight to behold. Prayer hands are visible on the outside of a vanilla cloud at this very moment. You want to see one? Pray for the cloud to appear before your very eyes, it will stagger you with so much everlasting beauty. This particular cloud just spun quickly. We have the opportunity to pray to the Lord to keep us safe from the harmful kind of spinning formations that come to destroy our lives with unwanted turmoil.

A creamy orange carnation is what the Lord studies down in front of His chest as He holds it inside of His hands. Honestly, He is doing just that and the flower turned into two! Jesus is holding them so close to His cheeks, it's hard telling if His face turned that beautiful color or if those flowers made them perfectly astounding. Not to say that His cheeks are not full of color already. He remarked, "They are close in color."

Instructed to talk about how hilly it is in heaven. They are turning gold and this is no surprise. It's funny when you can enjoy a good laugh and feel it spread inside of your tummy too. The Lord's people are yodeling on top of two large hills. "There are many nationalities who learn the talent," was the message from our spiritual teacher. "Hey there, guy. It's good to know us," a woman is saying as she too shows words of gold. Even though the man and woman appear to be a distance away on top of the hills, with their mouths working out a fresh tune between the gap between their hands, they lean in close from the spirit world too. They are covered in a very soft gold light. They try to message that during earlier times there were various ways to communicate across the land, and that included a long curling horn which was shown now. The woman expresses her thoughts which appear in black lettering while speaking through her hands. She said, "Goodbye." Very nice indeed and they will remain in memory as contributory.

This might sound weird but the interpreter always thanks the Lord, Father God, the Virgin Mary and all of the people in heaven who've been sending us messages, it just feels right. A four foot boy wearing a tall black entertainer's hat with a thin chin strap is disciplining both a lion and a strong looking elephant. It's interesting that they are powdery white, likely because of the Holy Spirit's soft light upon everyone. This is the word from the child of light. "My elephant is pink," said outright. Another look inside of the light proved he was telling the truth as the pink elephant was bouncing about. Either he has two pink elephants, otherwise the one he seems to be tapping with a prod has ran so fast that he or she appeared in two places. The elephant and lion don't at all feel any pain. "I entertain crowds often," the boy steps up from heaven and speaks his mind. The boy is really lively as he instantly turns into a very sparkly golden child.

While tiny sparkles of gold glitter cover his face he tapped something to his right and left, forming beautiful golden hearts. "Tell them the crowds I entertain are young and old alike. This child has just erased all fear of passing on into heaven. He said, "I am happy for everyone." He is very mature for his age. How can he be real? "You know there are children in heaven like me," the boy has spoken truthful so please believe. He feels there are ways for everyone to see him. "Look around for twinkling light," he included. He demonstrated touching a wand with more of a soft gold heart on the top reaching into the mystical golden tunnel of light before himself and many others today.

The spirit moves quickly without delay. Small building blocks have crumbled on the edges. It's suggesting stumbling blocks are easily removed with help from above. "Some people are very bashful about prayer," the Lord thinks inside of the light. People are dancing to Hawaiian sounds of music and sharing warm wishes. "Aloha, I come to you with hope," says a Hawaiian dancer wearing a white lei gently draped upon her shoulders. Her hair is very long and dark. She points out a beautiful white flower inside the lei and mentions, "Each color has meaning." In areas of heaven people are welcome with an "aloha" just like in Hawaii. "You have knowledge of us. We live to love each other," she explained. Her lei is mostly white, but she has many others of vibrant color. "I am pleased by your comments," she added to the conversation. There's another message about consuming some food items in heaven. And, one pig was shown all cooked as an example to go along with words which appear. Side by side two Hawaiian women have a white flower tucked into their hair, to where the flowers nearly touch, the ladies are identical in a way, loving friends inside of the white light. Maybe they do eat pig.

The Lord Jesus has an entertaining way of starting with colorful visions which are to be pieced together instead of being ignored. A black number one and a small blue mountain arrived within the specter of light and color. A pretty black lady draped in a long white robe has just had an immediate hair transformation. Her curly grey hair turned very dark. Another fine example how the other side works when arriving with streaks of silver and grey hairs on our head. No fault of our own it's just old age, but that won't last long, as we can see the woman in the spirit has changed, and not to forget, she stands holding a bouquet of white flowers with tinges of gold light shining upon them. It's a small bunch and very pretty. She looks like a flower girl all grown.

The interpreter is just waiting for someone to go flipping on through the air from the spirit world. That's funny, and not impossible for acrobats to do. "We can bounce as high as we want," a woman said, while exercising and wearing her full body suit in a soft peach color. The outerwear is lightweight with straps that extend over her shoulders. The image of her sitting upon her bottom with her stretching out to touch her fingertips to her toes seems very easy for her to do. "You know that we are very comfortable exercising," she said. It's a playful thing. Do people take showers in heaven? "We are very clean in heaven. You are causing laughter on our side from your question," the acrobatic woman tells the interpreter and all who are eager to listen.

"I came to visit you," Jesus says while appearing in the room. He looks awfully well. Jesus brings a smile and He has a way to make you feel as though you have a special gladness in your eyes when with Him. Jesus holds two thick gold candles in His hands with a flickering white light. They are feather light, and as He moves them up and down, one would believe He was weighing them in His hands. As this continues the candles become much smaller, but they glitter with white light embers. Silver halo's shining over the two candles.

A woman wearing ivory wings, says, "Time to work." "In heaven you will accept the way we have communion," Jesus expresses. The interpreter just silently asked, "Who was that from?" "Me was who," the Lord was the One speaking in a way to erase any doubts now. It's just thoughtful of the Lord to read your inner most thoughts inside of your mind. A man ready to tee off in heaven will hit the interpreter in the head with his golf ball if he does. Not really, but if you were facing him you'd think the same. A dark golf bag is standing straight, and the brightest white light known anywhere brightens beautifully. Either bring your own or you'll be given a new set of clubs to play with."We have fun playing golf," the player sends in a message from the greenest golf course ever. It is emerald green with plenty of rounded off areas where you'll have the chance to sink in your ball. The interpreter has never fully engaged in the sport, but as you see players in heaven such as "he" it becomes more inviting for us beginners. The scenery in the heavens on the course have been developed well. The Masters did a very good job.

The Holy Spirit is saying, "Wait until you are confident." The gentleness is great in the light. "You think there is too much violence in the streets. You are on the money," Jesus still speaks. Indirectly related that victims rewards are of great measure. The sun is glowing with strong rays of light upon just the softest pink angel ever. The golden halo is set in black interlaced design, and the entire gild has taken on its own shape of an angel wing. The halo itself. "I can teach you about the light," the angel has spoken, after comprising with the interpreter about something that would be confusing if carried on about. But, the angel has a way of guiding. A small black woven basket has white light glowing through the handle as the object rests upon a very bright golden stand, that's in between a "U-shape" on top, and with the connecting light holding it up, also one might believe it was in a "1" shape" too. The hoop handle was up high.

"Fill your basket up with warmth and love. You are very mature but need to grow still," the woman angel with the funny halo said. The pink angel was surprised at how well she was able to determine her size inside. "Expansion is very interesting," she tells the interpreter. "Ninety is old to you. Think about growing old and you will," the Holy Spirit makes this stunning announcement. That's strange because most people don't believe they'll even make it to that number or age. "If you are determined you will find a way to survive," was mentioned inside the spiritual realm. Again, the Lord's hands have sparkling gold rays of light darting upward in the heavens to where His face is illuminated. And He remains pleased.

Twinkling silver stars brighten inside of a blue background where a white sun or tunnel of light shoots out many rays that are transcending. All I can say is, "Mary lifts Her crown for adjustment, and with Her blue eyes, which are very soft, She watches over us now." That crown is still silver with encrusted diamonds. That mysterious ball of white light glows upon Her face, that which was originated from the center of Her crown, but you already knew where that came from. "It was a tulip like you thought," She says about the pretty yellow flower blooming inside of Her hand. She even instructs what to say. "It's nice to see you, Mary," expressed through prayer. "You behave like you should, just be wise with your talent," She explains to all of us. Mary created a huge heart shaped wreath filled with white flowers and raised it above Her Son's shoulders and head so He could wear it in heaven. "I believe you have everything right. My Mother is a very proud lady," the Lord expressed. The pink angel returned, and there was no mistaking her fancy halo. "I hope you like the Lord's wreath," she spelled out with words from the holy land of heaven. You'd think Mary would have said that, but it truly was from the angel.

We know there's something fishy going on here, but it isn't bad at all, it's factual that the Holy Spirit is still acting in such a kind way toward us today with messaging from the other side, we have the "Doubting Thomas" side of us coming out, because we haven't ever seen this continuing measure of the talkative side of Jesus and Mary, let alone from our higher power God. "I wish you would listen to the Virgin Mary more," Jesus advises. That's fine with us common folk, we'd love to hear much more from Her. Explore the spirit the best possible way that you can, whether you are sitting down or beginning to get up from your seat for a breather, expand your mind and let your spiritual eyes begin seeing the everlasting side of life.

Now from Mary we shall listen up again. And what a better time of the year to be associating ourselves with Her much more than ever before. Didn't we just hear from the Virgin Mary recently? Yes we did, but Her Son Jesus thought we should carry on under His and Her supervision. She must think that the interpreter is a little zany the way he acts. We sometimes have a secret side too. Let's keep it clean, even when we go a little bit overboard with our actions. Gold fragments of eternal light have appeared as being only those that have been made into two small lights from all of one. Where is Mary if the Lord wants us to pay heed once again?

"I am here with you," Mary says, while leaning over a tall yellow tulip. Her brown hair is more evident, and She had the right to remove Her crown. Her curling hair is not too wavy, nor is it that of a new hairstyle from the parlor. Her hair is still layered, rolling with those curls upon Her. The top of Her head is beautiful, such softness of beautiful brown hair. "I desire to touch Her softness even if it would be one fine moment in time to lay my hand upon Her head to pray," the interpreter thought about Mary's wonderful beauty from where he sits when watching Christ's Mother. The other garden behind her is filled with puffy white flowers. Oh how we could enjoy the day with Mary in Her gardens of beautiful flowers.

"You do have a way with words," Mary steps forward complimenting. Only a moment away from Mary and Her gardens. "We believe you enjoy the other side much more than many," I said unto you. Those were Mary's exact words in the Holy Spirit. But how can that be true if we are here and all of the people who have died and have gone on are enjoying the blissful side of heaven now? She meant that heaven is appreciated by many of us who are faithful to Her.

"Bless you dear one," Mary is saying. A gold light shines on the interpreter. Mary feels love towards us. Her messages had better be told now. From a pea size mint green circle of light Mary expands the same color vibration to a huge widening pathway, there in which She rests inside of the warmth of euphoria on a good side view which She has taken. Upon Her throne very well-balanced She can be seen. "It was a little bit difficult to see me at first," Mary declares. Her silver crown stood out as did She, but Mary was in the mint green light mostly all covered, leaving Her spirited self still known. Now don't go running and pack all of your bags up to come see the Virgin Mary appear inside of the interpreter's home for healing and all of your other needs, She can visit you right at this very moment.

"Remember to wish upon a falling star," Mary relates in the spirit world. It's fascinating that She can keep visiting at the drop of the hat. Mary changed Her appearance to where She was visible here in a very enlarged white robe. She looked pregnant. "Use Jesus as an example. My Son was a very special birth for me," She says with dignity. She feels that many people are puzzled why they can't see visions clear enough. Think about praying first then messages will be clearer. But you can trust everything said still. "I miss seeing you, Greg," the interpreter's mother just told him in an instant message from heaven, a place where she lives freely. Yes Mother's Day is here and it will be gone at the end of the night, but we will always know in our hearts that our family living above us will always be very close to us in spirit. "I'm just glad it wasn't a ton of tears coming from myself, but the teardrop that did come was comforting, the comfort which comes from knowing "mom" came through the light too. You can see your mother visit, it's not hard. Seek and you shall find out for yourself how close she is.

Now try looking for your mother in the spirit world. "I'm going to assist you," Mary says, known by Her words appearing inside of the holy realm, which is not that far from your own reach. A special lesson from Mary on how to reach your mom right now. "Begin by reaching out to me. Don't be afraid of the Virgin Mary," She says politely. She would have you think about the last time you saw her. We are talking about contacting her in a new life still. The warmth in her heart is the same. "Let the visions flow directly to you. Peek around white light," Mary seems to be saying. "You'll know when she comes," Mary is looking upon you now, knowing you'll be praying for light. "Ask me to guide you and I will bring your mother into your home," Mary would like you to believe. She helped a lot. At times your mother will appear next to the Lord. You'll want to go to their side. That's how glad you'll feel when you see your own kind come within the Holy Spirit. Wow was Mary ever present just now. Hail Mother Mary!

Why is the invisible moving around in here so much today? It seems God and the Lord have a huge right to our well-being, as much or more than we have for ourselves. The Holy Spirit held back a little. Let's hope they are not planning to catapult something into the air. Movement as such as to be winding up. "You really know the aspects of the Holy Spirit. We feel for you when you hesitate about us," Jesus clarifies. The Lord points to a person's arms. They were being rubbed. "It's helpful to protect your skin," He advises in heaven. The sun isn't scorching up there, it's down here on earth. It has been advised to be cautious at times because your skin may burn while sunbathing. Lotion wiggled out from a tube into a woman's hand and before you know it, she is here from heaven exhibiting for us with her hands close to her face, that she has applied some to her skin for reason. "Don't neglect your health," she said. She really did visit, or we had visited with her if you will. The interpreter said, "I believe all of this." If you don't believe in the spirituality in heaven which is already around you, then who will? Everything must count when this positive.

They didn't just show two scalps, one very red and burned, and the other top of someone's head healthy? Yes they did. It seemed they were finished talking about burning your skin out in the sun. "You should be careful because of the history with melanoma," was expressed through divine intervention. Someone inside of our reading group just received an unexpected surprise then. Who else was the Lord talking about?

A tiny gold cross appeared across the room. They are cute if you catch a glimpse of one quickly. The Holy Spirit says, "The Dutch really think you have special writing." Well that's very interesting, although it is all about our Lord Jesus, not a theory on "what could be" or "what may have been." Wherefore your Lord has been presenting you with the facts of life.

The Lord appears in a mild gold light which you knew He would do. The interpreter thought, "Not candles again!" We can't stop Him from showing us His beautiful candles with holy light. So it was "my bad." The smile on the Lord's face is huge. You'd swear He just ate a piece of delicious apple pie. That kind look. Why does He show a huge crusted pie after saying that about Him? He is giving the impression, with that sliced piece now removed from the pie that He's enjoying a little bit of the fruits from His labor. This is no lie, there's a small amount bitten off from the tip of the piece. Jesus is showing an example of two people eating pie. One person's cheeks are jammed full of food, while the other person can be seen with a lesser amount inside his mouth. It's obvious by watching them chew, and you can tell by how big their cheeks were. Apparently we shouldn't be overeating. A very happy person says, "I like pie." He's happier than Santa. He said, "You can join us later." We should take him up on that, he's holding pie that looks super delicious.

The Indians are coming. At least they are here. The long headdress full of white feathers runs from the top of the honored chief's head down close to the ground. "I'd rather not have it touch the ground," the proud Indian says. The interpreter's eyes widen, surprised by the strong presence. It's not true, "if you've seen one Indian, you've seen them all." He's shaking orange light around in his hand, to where the shooting color brightens high and then low. Therefore, his hand is shaking it about, but he is dancing a little. He stopped that activity for the moment at hand as Jesus is whispering into his ear something important. We better find out what He said. "What did you say, Jesus?" asked the interpreter. "There's plenty of time to know about Indians and the truthful nature of their being," Jesus is assuring us. The interpreter thought, "What?" Time seems to be a no-no to us when speaking of heaven, but apparently Jesus is the timekeeper who is keeping track of every second within our existence, whether be up in heaven or down here on earth. A woman here is pointing down to a vanilla tunnel of light. It's a small tunnel or ball of eternal presence. Probably the tunnel way down there. How it was perceived as she sits here in the room right now. Bigger than the biggest person seen in a long, long time. She is pointing to her nasal where a small bag of white powder has levitated in front of her. The word "habit" appeared in black lettering. The interpreter doesn't need a bad habit like that, nor does anyone else. "We think it's better if you stayed away from drugs," the kind lady suggested.

"You find yourself wondering more about the inside of the kingdom," the Holy Spirit pointed out. "You will enjoy what I have here."

"The healing feels wonderful for you. There are people feeling the warmth of the Holy Spirit inside of their souls when they think about healing," both God and Jesus say. Jesus or God is the One in the spirit world right now raising His right had, palm up, one level at a time, and then He lowers it to help with the intended message. "Raise the Lord up, but remember my Father will help too," Jesus said in earnest. And the word "okay" could be seen. Isn't Jesus everything for you? He is always there to help the confused too.

What are the brown cardboard boxes open for? We really hope not to be moving to heaven all of a sudden. A small white garment on a hanger of light raised up from inside of the box on the left. "We will provide your clothing still," Father God assures. His name was seen, therefore, He is God. "Children have had misfortune like you think," came from above.

Do you recall people making little ghosts out of cloth, attaching a string or wire to them to make them bounce up and down? Likely in movies, but the Holy Spirit moves even much more swifter. A man in the spirit world has his right hand tucked inside of his waistcoat. Looking like a soldier from earlier times, you can imagine who he was. It seems he went way back in time. "You should know I am him," the friendly spirit said, using language familiar to the interpreter. It is just hard to say that it was Napoleon. Any ways he took off that superb honey of a big hat from his head and bowed before us in the spirit. Trying to bow back to him with a little shock running through the interpreter's mind, a relaxed feeling arose when doing so. Anything is possible.

"Overall the final conclusion is to love you forever," Jesus said, because He's now here in the interpreter's livingroom, humbly looking down, and is He ever blessed with healthy hair growth. "Don't give up my friend," He said. That's Him alright, and that's how our good Lord speaks. Praise the Lord for everything. Hendrix! "Peace my friend. I can play for you in heaven," spoken. Hard to believe? He was just here inside of the Holy Spirit. Now that's powerful. First Jesus then Hendrix. Magnificio!

Pointed out in two spots. The vanilla gold colored halos appeared very rounded. Followers of Christ, because the children are Godly, and not more than a few years in age. Ascending gradually through the heavens, why not call them little twins? They have white glow sticks, because that's what they've been holding, and believe me, they would be excellent guides to begin following on our journey inside of heaven. There have been other youngsters who have been exciting to hear about, but these two are way up there in their own class of people.

The children think they are the ones who are "delighted" to visit. Why did the word "Swedish" appear? These kids must have parents and grandparents from Sweden. Still ascending the children are in plain view. They want to visit the same way as with the interpreter. Many children now appear in a swarm. If the interpreter had known all along this many little ones were protecting us in heaven, there wouldn't be any need for worry. Funny how the small angelical children come with a protective spirit of guardianship when very near. It seems if anyone were to cross their path they would encircle them immediately. Develop your own awareness of them standing or kneeling. They were in a large circle in mid-air, and now the children are in the aforementioned position. Likely for your benefit. A little angel's nose turned all red, then became very normal. The child is a small girl with shoulder length brown hair. She wanted us to believe her when she said, "I don't have colds anymore." Truthful words visible to the naked eye for interpretation.

Have you had any lucid dreams lately where words became visible to you, either on storefronts, plaques, or on any other item? You see how the interpreter reminds everyone how easy it is to view wording inside of the holy messages received. One way or another the Lord will get His spiritual messages sent through to us without delay.

While wondering if there was anything more important, it dawned on the interpreter that there wasn't anything or anyone more important than the children of heaven. "We believe you have found a deeper meaning to life," the Lord delivered in a message. Two blue spots of light brighten. There are other angelical children in the background, where their presence has become known from three orange flames of light in the foreground. The children are nearly the same age at fifteen and sixteen according to the Holy Spirit. They stand in a tight circle singing and rejoicing in the Lord and our Father God. Their faces brighten from the orange illumination. "We found victory in the Lord," a young man said, and you wouldn't believe in a million years what he did. Go ahead and guess. While looking at a trio the young man with light brown hair was bent over at a real keyboard, identical to the interpreter's. Therefore, he wanted the interpreter to step it up and place to print what he was saying. His words came, and he was determined to have them shared with the rest of us. Kind of unreal, but it's true.

A dark steam engine is letting off grey smoke, although the Holy Spirit wiped it clean from view as fast as it came here. "Cool down when you feel mad," instructed by the Lord saying so. Thought about what He had said. The Lord moves four spaces quickly to where His holy vibration was seen. The number four appeared after Him moving around in heaven. He said, "What would you say if you had four days left to live on earth?" "Good Lord!" from the interpreter and more thanks to God and for Mary being such wonderful spiritual people. That's the interpreter's thoughts on them, and there's no doubt that many people will feel that God, Mary and Jesus are in fact spirits. "Don't worry we realize how you feel," from Jesus. The spiritual world is a habitant of spiritual people who cherish every second in the light. Jesus personally brought this up in conversation while reflecting on the other side of life.

People are very surprised by the gift to contact their loved ones. The interpreter will concentrate on people coming through the spirit world to see if there's anyone who'll need contacting over here on our side. In other words, by meditating keenly in the spirit the interpreter will attempt to contact your loved ones. Who knows better than spirit people? A man in all white stands here very tall. A collie dog is with him. He says, "Bill is okay." "Move on now," Jesus instructed. There will be at least seven contacts regarding listeners, those who should recognize their family from above. Others may contact their family members through prayer, and instantly they should appear before you. Just keep on trying. Now on with the remaining six messages.

A woman by the name of Violet is present. She has nice brown hair which is full. A small violet flower is near her face. She spelled out her name, but furthermore her soft movement from her lips, expressive as she was, she also became known by from reading her lips. The woman feels you shouldn't feel sorrowful by her being away. The Holy Spirit verifies everything that is heard and said in His name.

"Begin with a visitor from heaven," the spirit side of life suggests. Well she is quite cute with a sparkly gold bow on the side of her head, was created for beauty as it's a seemingly loose fit inside of her auburn hair. "Hi! I didn't mean to interrupt your spiritual reading," she came out saying. She's doing just fine. She holds a glowing white candle and the base in which it is secured to swirls. All in white. "My parents wonder about what my living conditions are like. Splendid indeed!" she sends to some very special people on her mind. More to come. "The Lord is a perfect gentleman and a good friend of mine. The people think it is true, but are unsure why," she believes. Two boomerang like arches of white light move in perfect measure when forming. "I have passed over into the light is why you saw those," she said, and that is so far unbelievable that it is still absolutely true. One way she'll get her direct message across is by her standing near her Pekinese. Glad for that bit of insight from her. "I will give you a hint to tell them what is going on over here with me," the lady says. God bless her soul it's time to visit more people.

A pipe smoker with knee problems comes in being very savvy. "Your reader will understand who I am," he said by showing dark wording. The interpreter's jaw drops. "Meeting you is a pleasure my friend. Would you believe I am free to be me?" our gentleman says proudly. And now this. "When I was younger I enjoyed golfing on the greens," he mentions. So what's the deal with him now? Does he still golf like others whom we've had such a great honor understanding more about with that sportive event going on in heaven? "You better your bottom dollar," he immediately says. He read the interpreter's thoughts, and somehow the interpreter believed that the visiting member of Christ's heavenly family is looking over his shoulder helping. "There is a process here that you will often enjoy," he doesn't fail to mention to us. Within white light he is soft, and the man's facial expression is priceless. How do people get to be that fortunate? What a guy! So happy and peaceful was he, a man who has contacted a family member or members, in a most unorthodox manner.

Much better than going to an important engagement at the theater. A hand in the spirit was revealing five fingers, if you count the thumb. You know what that means? We have guest number five coming in from heaven. There was a real hand visible, not floating inside of the air, it was suspended inside of the Holy Spirit. A darling of a young lady not really that tall. Her eyes twinkle with a little white light and silver reflections against her dark brown eyes. Short straw blonde hair belongs to the young lady. So very delicate. She grasps her hands, and she says, "Pray for peace." A pinkish white angel's wing comes out of the blue and the image was absolutely delightful. She has a special talent for her friends to notice. She draws attention to the golden ball of light in front of her chin. With her mouth moving the ball of light it sends a circular halo around her head bringing a great golden existence. The halo disappears when the white ball of light appeared beneath her chin now. She controlled which ball of light should shine beneath her chin. She creates in a new halo forming a nice white arch of light around her head, the same way, but with unusual tactic. "My brother would know me immediately. We argued too much tell him," she was talking sense. She had a neck injury. "I think you will get through to him a little," she communicated from her home in heaven. Hopefully her brother will stop and think.

Gleaming gold cuffs to a special robe made for a little lady are admired by her, but that tail to her garment was examined closer yet with her deep appreciation of the very fine beauty it holds within. She bends only slightly and holds it between her fingers the white and golden flowers along the hem. She twirls inside her gown and as she does one white flower and one gold petaled beauty left the hemline and landed in her hands. She loves their scent. "It is magic to you what happened. Enjoy watching me," she tells us. Three red carnations arch off into an angel wing. She seems surprised by her expression at what she has done, but we know that she is influencing us in the heavens. "Son, I am ok, don't fret. It was my time to leave your side," the friendly spiritual woman is saying. So we know she has a child on our side who must be listening in on the conversation otherwise she wouldn't be present.

She is instructing that her pet's collar had some sparkling silver. The interpreter sees a white dog with a brown patch of fur upon the animal's face. There might be some black fur upon the dog's face as well. It appears that way when coming in much clearer for observation. "The rock specimen was what we saw when we went camping," she is explaining about sparkling rocks of many colors that appeared on her side too. She looks at the interpreter with an expression of, "I guess you believe me, I hope that my son does too." She's in peace, and with that expression she makes one wonder a lot about how people feel in heaven. Many exact feelings as we do, and exceptionally well everlastingly.

"Greater numbers will be contacted indirectly," the Holy Spirit advises the interpreter, topping what was said about seven people coming in through the spirit to become closer with their beloved. Whatever they say is good, but it could mean people from all walks of life may be routing messages too. A dark pathway suddenly disappears because the Lord would have us walk on one much brighter full of life. "I am concerned too," the Lord says as He believes there is much needed effort in contacting Him. It doesn't mean a strain on the brain, but more involvement with meditation. Small rings of white glowing light may be sought after in your presence. The Lord will reveal even more once you locate these vibrant visions of light. Fuller visions will come forth when doing so. It will seem as though angels pop up suddenly. How did an angel come out from inside of that glowing ring? The wings sort of just unfold from the rings of light and there you have them in your presence all at once. If you visualize them in front of you a few feet away down on the floor, just search for the small circles of them to begin shedding light. The circles are not full of gleaming light until you have your mind set on them for you to see each one clear. Once you have one or more of them in sight they will fill out. Multi-color baby angels and their halos if you are lucky.

The youngster is a boy on a tricycle and he has white wings. "Mom, I love you," he expresses while stopping to say hi to her from heaven. His words were in white letters which were quite readable. The best message of all came from this little tyke on his trike.

What's really frustrating is expecting wonderful results all the time and we get handed a raw deal. We should still rely on God and His Son. If things don't seem to be working out, we just go into a new area with their guidance. New direction is needed. "An intelligent person just walked by," the Lord spoke of someone who was drawn in by the interpreter, while looking out the window at her now. Us men can do more than one thing at a time. Funny how the Lord commented on another passerby. Oh good Lord. "You were cute as a button when you were a child, Greg," the interpreter's mother, Dorothy, just said such a cute thing from inside of the Holy Spirit. She is with the Lord and was mentioned because of the close contact established mostly. Who would deceive the Holy Spirit and his own mother to gain recognition? Not here in this camp.

"You're going through troubling times yourself but will come out smelling like roses," another comment came in the spirit with a beautiful yellow rose appearing. While not knowing a hundred percent if cancer may be growing inside of the body, the Holy Spirit says, "Believe the Lord has a miracle waiting. You are selfish at times," Jesus mentions to the interpreter and there you have it, a normal human being after all. Being an interpreter in the spirit, able to see on both sides of life daily is very unusual, but so stupendous that there's no amount of gold you could offer in trade for the gift. Two sparkling silver candles inflame with yellow pointy light from their own wicks.

There are yellow and white rainbows in heaven along with the very colorful arcs of vibrant colors which we are aware of. At first one child was seen hugging a mild yellow color rainbow, until many more children were visibly wrapping themselves inside of the huge crescent, which suddenly turned into churning clouds, softer than anything ever seen in life before. Baby white creased angel wings are popping up from inside of the creation now. "I'm watching them,"the Lord is saying while sitting in front of the kids, while very happy upon His throne within a very fine glistening gold light. The kids appear to be bouncing about when moving all around inside of the yellow spiraling cloud of eternal light, that which was originally a solid yellow rainbow. Either the lad or Jesus began the rotation inside of the arc. So very happy are they in heaven. Jesus is busily stretching His white sleeved arms outward helping children by lifting their spirits up. The rotating yellow light turned back to an ordinary arc of light now.

The day has become much better with troubling times barely existing anymore. One small incident shouldn't ruin one's entire life, that's just how it is. Seeing Jesus playing around with His tiny children was really wonderful, and since we know the Lord like we do, we will often see a repeat of how He manages to take care of so many of them congregated near and around Him. "My children are celebrating every day with my Son because of His name," God has managed to send to you in a message today. God really is amazing, even if He is hanging His head down right now. In the white spiritual light, His image is like the Lord's for many good reasons, and it is known why He is doing what He is doing. He wasn't looking for clams, He had the disappointing look on His face, only as an example of how He may be thinking some of us have felt on days when things should have gone much better. He is benevolent. God is understanding our pain, and takes on an image that He feels we might be kindred to. Or, He places Himself in our shoes. He even laughs at the way we think. "True, from our viewpoint," the Holy Spirit interjected. Jesus is about to say something. The interpreter doesn't know why Jesus keeps coming here inside of the Holy Spirit, but maybe it's because He loves him too.

"You have toiled through many hard times. I want the best for you, always," He actually just said to us. Does that sound good enough to hear from the Lord after working many long years through your life? "Your rewards have been few on your side, but will be of many when you come home to the Lord," honestly, the Lord is showing descriptive words in the spirit, which He just hath said. He should be highly commended.

Cheerful children with rosy cheeks peek over very pearly dish stands of clear water, where they see things, and even people in them. That will be explained. One of the children sends his words. "I can see where you are from here. I know you miss your family," he says, and it's way beyond the interpreter's knowledge how and why he is so smart and understanding of someone he has never met before. Remarkably at his young age it is a miracle in disguise that a small child who holds up one hand, relating that he is "five" can do so much for all of us. And you never know how broken hearted you really are until you deeply think of how much you miss everyone who has left your world. The kids look great. They even come in better through the light, and likely on account of the acceptance we have for them. Even without really knowing these children well, we are so very adult in our minds to hope they have everything special for themselves. Beautiful apricot and golden color light sparkles in heaven where these children are. One of the children sends a message reading: Special Greetings.

"You wonder about the dishes, what kind of mysteries are held within the living waters of life," the Lord seems to be saying as He planned out the event with the children, there within the heavens where He is actively enjoying the signs. Some will think it's a mystery how it was told, and how everything has happened. Soft blue light approaches.

A straight pearl necklace is laced inside of a gold light. A very fine string of pearls. Now pearls form in a couple of arches, one for a singular angelic wing, and the other made a fancy halo. A face comes through. The angel is female who sits upon a huge mound of unstrung pearls. Her face and the background is colored very vanilla, not like ice-cream, but more of the shade identical to paper. Between white and tan mostly. She holds one pearl between her fingers and lets it drop below to the pile beneath her. It turned into two white tears. Suddenly all of the pearls beneath her changes to white dots. She sits back and those white dots form a smaller platform beneath her, as it tilted as well, she is ascending up into the heavens. She was launched in a very soft manner. That would explain the three small platforms that were thought to be visible. One for sure, but after viewing it move backward and then reverberate as such, then the final conclusion was that it was only one small platform sending her off to new heights. It is possible to see a one wing angel. If you believe you will see her then you have the right to, too.

Again, the Lord desires accuracy with His messages. A line of blue, yellow and pink eternal light radiated. Rusty red brown and gold mixes together and it shines. Dark black with white and green small stripes appear side by side. A lot of colors that is for sure. It felt as though someone just slid in to our side on a slide, the motions were clear. Unless, there is a super long pussycat's tail in the spirit. Time to look up again to see. They're just too much. In the shape of a kite there are four angelical cutties across from each other with one at the bottom, and the other child above in the four sided arrangement as well. And you guessed it, their hands tucked softly beneath their chins which makes you feel they have been mapping out this visit. New children of the grand spirit world. What can these children tell us that the other angels haven't already? Joy, peace happiness and love were the words in sparkling gold beneath each child. One message from each of God's little helpers. "Tell them messages are real from the angels," was told. If you thought it was old news you would be wrong. Sparkling gold everywhere.

"I couldn't agree more," the Holy Spirit said through word language coming in from the other side of life. In regards to silent thought there is nothing worse than missing your children. Many white liberty bells sit in a white hub, although a very large bell comes in very pink, and white light is more adjoined to them now. "Many people are worried," the Lord speaks about one's personal freedom in life. You are going to think everything is really exciting to you when you arrive in heaven. The freedom you'll receive will make you think twice.

It was guessed at that the interpreter was seeing two hotdogs on their buns. They were yellow in the light. Maybe we can eat them in heaven? "We will forbid that for a reason," was related back and without hast that food item will not be permitted. In the past the Lord has shown fruits would be suitable for consumption. Jesus appeared just now. His face is so colorful. That was said before, but really, how ingenious of God to have the Lord return to perfect health and then some. "There is a reason for divine intervention," Jesus said plainly to hear, downright straight forward with all sincerity. He believes we shouldn't rush so much.

Four red strawberries appear in a square. The Lord says, "Your health will improve." There is help on the horizon. Why the state of Texas came into view from the Lord was for teaching us what problems exist that He is fully aware of, such as the ongoing drought. Maybe the state will have some much needed rain, hopefully. Mentioned in the light, "People pray for rain." What good will that do? Let's see what the Holy Spirit says about praying for rain to come. "Do you actually believe people can pray for rain and actually receive it, Jesus?" asked by the interpreter. "Faith works wonders son," Jesus responded nicely. Jesus even comments on the poor state of economy in Illinois in America. "Your state is on the mend but it will take time," were the Lord's exact words translated clearly. "What about some good news for the many countrymen and women of different countries around the world?" asked in prayer while the Lord and Father God listens. There is peace.

"Speak freely from me to the people. I am present," Jesus explained. The country of Italy appears with the name spelled out across the map of it. "You'll be skeptic, but tell them anyway," the Lord commanded. That's the problem with being an interpreter of the Holy Spirit, one must be a little skeptical when observing in order to set things right, because it's a must to think things through first, just in case there's a huge fat error.

"What about Italy?" asked. "They deserve to be spoken of. They're known for their home life and cooking," said from the Lord's point of view. "They're honored up here." There's an Italian chef popping up over here on our side. That mustache and happy face is good to see. "Anthony is my name," spoken in a cool way. "Hello Anthony," said with folded hands and a silent meditation, while the translating interpreter does his best. With a tall white chef's hat on his head he seems to be joking around about the fresh loaf of bread held high in his left hand, so much as to be stretching his arm nearly behind himself too. He couldn't be keeping that yummy bread from us now. "We are preparing life for you. Italy is going to surprise many other countries in the future," Anthony says it's so, so it must be true. One other thing. "Of course you can eat bread in the spirit," our Italian chef means what he says, and he also circled his finger and thumb to signal everything was okay.

"Lord Jesus, how about Belgium?" asked right off the top of the interpreter's head how well they'll do. "They really know chocolate. I love everyone. There is unrest at times but faith will overrule all things that are troubling,"Jesus declared inside of His Holy Spirit. Unbelievable, yet the Lord is a good King. "Flemish are proud people," Jesus also mentions, and it is certain of that He has all of the same full regard and utmost respect for everyone living in the great land of Belgium. "Netherlands is close by," Jesus can't help but saying in His devoted messaging. Thought ahead of time, and it's nice He brings "visible wording in the spirit to be translated."

"I'm especially fond of them. But I think of everyone the same," saith the Lord, and His Father God wanted to be included within this message of love. That was terrific. "Germany is special too," from messaging. The country Ireland will be spoken of. First the country appeared, then one of those cute magical leprechauns popped up, seemingly jumping all around in excitement. And you'll think it was crazy, but that elf guy had a pipe in his mouth. "We can help you out there, friend," someone in the light said, and it looks like a blonde man with gleaming green eyes. If he isn't Irish we better declare him one of the people from Ireland. He tips a black derby which he holds beneath his chin. So close in fact that the brim is gently touching his chin now. "You should continue on talking about the people of the world," he ensured, because of the accuracy and holiness of the spiritual messages effecting one another one way or another.

The name Argentina appeared, but the interpreter knows absolute nothing about the people living there. "Special people live within the region. The people are loved dearly," Jesus just spoke of them. There was mention about Africa. "You think they are very poor people. I want Africa's people to love one another," Jesus speaks of inside of His holy realm during this very moment. It's not fake, the Lord is speaking right now. "People think it's an unusual gift, but will know the truth has been spoken," the Lord said. "Canadians have a lifestyle which is rich," that was a far-reach to Canada, but the interpreter really appreciates the way the Lord wastes no time in directly communicating. "Let the Holy Spirit decide who should be named. I appreciate your help as an interpreter," Jesus says. Do you know how much that means?

"I will tell you many great things," the Lord seems so remindful. Two small boys facing the opposite direction, wearing white angelical robes which swoop down in the back are holding glowing candles. They have dark hair and the boys are a guiding light according to the Lord. Their candles are almost foggy white, except for the light on top which is very clear. Even as they look away from each other, somehow we can't help believing that they are still being guided into the right direction overall. "Peace from Jesus," another quick sign. Oh no are they all finished with spiritual signs and wonders for those of us who choose to study their messages? "You know we will always help the people on your side," God relates. His name was seen when looking up to see who was speaking using the special English language. "We prefer to send you messages this way," was shown and spoken of positively.

"It would help if you didn't have salt," communicated to here. That last message came when thinking about going out to buy some chips and dip. Enough to make one start chewing down on some tough leather. That really did hurt. They are trying to tell the interpreter to do things in moderation which can be difficult when it comes to foods so well-liked. "You have a stubborn quality inside," Jesus is saying. The good Lord knows. "Half as much is possible," He says. But have you ever sat down to eat just a few chips and dip? Being at the proper weight is helpful and is sometimes an excuse to eat more, but that salt could kill a person's body over time. Can you imagine going to heaven and God sits down with you discussing the real reason why you had died at such a young age that it was because of eating the wrong foods? "You will be well-informed why you came to us," the Lord steps in to say. While sitting here in hesitation, the Lord says, "You have a special talent in getting our message through to people." Heard before, from the Lord's lips to the interpreter's ears. However, it is a huge undertaking, one that will go down in history for the interpreter, should no one care to ever believe in what the Lord and his holy family in heaven are saying, which is likely not the case, but if it were to be, the interpreter would still know of the enormity of the Lord's will. "Let it be," was another message.

A swift downward motion suggests perhaps a drummer in the spirit world is having loads of fun. Three huge drums rest in front of musicians who bask inside of a white and gold tinted heavenly light, when conversing joyfully like it's a normal thing to do. We are so in for a big surprise when we get to heaven. But wait, we're there right now in spirit. The drums go off to the left and right some, while the one in the middle of the group is still well-centered. What is the name of that drumstick with the furry white ball attached to it? Any ways, one of them is levitated while slanting without movement, and it was decorated with a small gold bow beneath the rounded ball. "Don't worry what others are thinking," said in the spirit of things happening. That has been said before, so we know now that every little sign comes from heaven after all.

Two red poppies fill the air with a creative sense. A wiggly golden light. Soft pearl vases hold one white flower inside each one of them. They appear everywhere. An affectionate symbol realized. A pure gold chest opens with more of God's golden coins shining brightly. Black letters appear which read: Ask in my name. Go ahead and ask the Lord and God for money, health and riches. The interpreter found it somewhat hard to believe himself, but if that is the way they see it in heaven then so be it. "You'll be helpful to people," the Lord says.

The interpreter is aware of a strategy that the Lord and God uses at times. They'll have more fun with us when we are more in sync with them. Two hands appear wearing white gloves. That's right, just the hands are visible, gloved. The hands are very tight fisted. Take your time. The interpreter is supposed to let the people figure it out. What the Lord did show was that His index fingers crossed one another. He made a special cross with white gloves on. Unless that wasn't the Lord. "You took the right approach," the Lord must be saying, because spelled out words read that.

A dark red structure to a wide castle appeared at a very eerie dimension. The word "crumbled" appeared. "The devil is more of a lost cause," the Holy Spirit spoke about during this message of images and words. Several shades of blue are evident. A hot red crescent looked as if someone could burn themselves by touching it. Why would that appear in heaven? "The light is a powerful source," declares the Lord. A glowing pink candle is tall and beautiful. Mesh ivory angel wings that become huge rise slowly. "We guard ourselves here," Jesus speaks truthfully. "There are thousands of ways to travel around heaven." Those messages just came so quickly.

We will even whirl around slowly or smoothly if you prefer. An orangish gold cloudy formation sounds silly to travel through, but why is someone peeking out from a similar structure with the segments of cloudiness balled up into several small groups of clouds? "You should explore the Holy Spirit," the traveler relates, and you can only groove to someone like that with such great knowhow. As light as air, every movement considered, the Lord wraps up the colorful cloudy forms and appears standing in His white robe. "I send my love to everyone today. The will of my Father is planned," also politely said. When Jesus meant there were thousands of ways to move throughout the spirit world, He must have in mind the various directions to take, besides how our inner soulful spirit of ourselves will turn about using methods in traveling about inside of His kingdom.

A golden chariot appeared, and we shall know how they were used through lectures. Will we ride in one? It has quite a lot of appeal, the one presented in the light. They are trying to say, "We can accommodate you with a ride." The steps we take when moving forward won't be difficult as though we were climbing steep hills with large footsteps, but the steps will almost seem like we are walking on clouds. White footwear pointing upward and suddenly more flat upon a puffy white cloud is telling to the naked eye and an open mind now. The Lord appreciates us knowing the different approach we will be taking when walking.

Blue light appears with sparkling silver enlightening one's eyesight. A vibrant yellow scooter is parked sideways, at least with the wheel turned in such a direction. To speak in behalf of the Holy Spirit, we can drive or ride them upon selected roadways in heaven. Not necessarily ran with motor gas though. Magically they will run casually for our enjoyment mainly. It will be breezy but very nice outdoors on the other side. "You can ride around all day for fun," a young man is saying, as he can be seen upon a scooter with raised arms in the air. He's in a smooth vanilla color of light which is very beautiful and calming. Let's hope he is parked, unless he is riding freely without any hands on the wheel, which may be safe for him, after all he is in heaven where no one will ever be harmed.

"We are very concerned with children passing into the light, but we may converse openly," the Holy Spirit was saying. Communications with the Lord this way is the best church ever experienced with the interpreter attending on time for a change. It's very strange to the interpreter that ministers around the world don't have such a gift to be so in touch with the other side. "There are many who have feelings about us, but they fall short of the message at times. Use your intuitive side to prosper now," Jesus clearly explains in the spirit. The more difficult the message the more inclined we are to be non-believers. So don't expect Jesus and God to be overly sophisticated when messaging. "There are thinkers among you who are worrying about dying. Fret no longer, I am with you throughout time," a spiritual message from the Lord resting inside of calm white light, while He seems to be studying an open book before Him.

The word "Bible" sparkles in all gold. "Praise the Lord," words presented in the spirit, therefore the interpreter said the same thing knowing the Lord is listening to us when we do praise His name. Say it softly or sing praise to them loudly, our heavenly Father and the Lord hear every whisper that comes from our lips. Don't worry about not remembering everything they have been telling us, the ability to know everything precisely will come in the hereafter where we will have amazing thoughts about everything ever known and all that becomes real. But we can refer to their spiritual transcripts anytime we feel like going over the material set forth, and all which we have come to believe in. Keep as much in your memory as possible.

The Lord and His Father certainly are spiritual builders. All of the activity is ongoing, also somewhat of a mystery at times. Funny how the Lord's spirituality suggested two small black lines close to meeting together, somewhat intensely they nearly pinched each other. Moments later the interpreter's kneecap felt an excruciating pain, not something that happens often. That's where we need to continue watching each sign associated with the Holy Spirit. "Should I look up again?" the interpreter questions if and when he should. You know why? In such a peaceful state of what came to him, the mind sort of just absorbs such a beautiful wonder which had arrived, and obviously will stay as long as we are interested. Sworn to the greater power above us, small children must be walking around in this blissful state of heavenly bliss, because real dark flowers are drifting around in the air, and you know there's more to be revealed once the interpreter examines the rest of the apparitions. "Children are present like you were thinking. The flowers are in memory of people who love you," Jesus laughs about while He relates this outwardly now.

An intense smile is just as nice, or can be even nicer, than a very peaceful loving face. You can be very happy about that message. "It was who you thought," our Lord says. Let's put it like this in simpler expressions. Your loved ones cling onto the light, and have came unto the Lord, but in an unexpected visitation they'll express deep sadness before we begin to cry, all from their unexpected presence on this side with them visiting, only because of the greater forbearance which they feel inside their heart for you. Your loved ones should be visiting if you will only look up and expect someone to be smiling, perhaps after what will be noticeably a "sadness" in their expression. Not always the case, but often it seems this tends to help you understand that they respect that inner sorrow due to such a great loss. Foreseeing two yellow tulips will also bring you closer to them. That's what the spirit shows.

A white fist with a leather belt wrapped around was an obvious message. But, when the Lord spoke using visible wording He confirmed our beliefs. "When you were younger you were disciplined by your mother with the belt. She realizes it would have been better to have waited," spoken about in the Holy Spirit. Someone in the land understands what the Lord just related about strict discipline with children. That was a natural way of life many years ago to pull out the belt and let all hell break loose if the kids got out of hand, but not anymore. Your mother has sent you a message from the other side of life. They feel it will clear your mind.

"A ghostly apparition just then, but it was peaceful," Jesus describes. It was a black veil dragging across the floor with an expansion of the Holy Spirit removing it from sight. "I am aware of the spooky side to spirits. We are considered the Holy Spirit," spoken just right. A yellow flower lays flat stemming from an attractive white light. The bottom of the stem touches inside of the light, to where about an inch of it humped up.

"Try to be sensible," the message from the other side. A very thin arch over the Lord's head is accompanied by much revealing white light. So very enticing. Truthfully the whole account of what the Lord and His loyal family in heaven have been relating to us has taken a little bit of time, but without much of a long intermission between messages, that is from day to day. And, the Lord still appears in front of the interpreter, around him, and often in the midst, where He has promised to be for all of His children on the planet. "Prove it if you need to. All it takes is a small amount of faith," the Lord speaks of. Look close to your feet, small ivory angels line up in the unfolding of one large wing. When you look for them, you'll then know what the interpreter is talking about. Don't be afraid just be calm. A large blue wing is appearing in very commanding white light, so that may be seen when looking forward. You'd think the white light would be brighter, and it is in heaven, but if hard to understand, wait until the light brightens.

"God bless the sick children, Lord," a prayer just said, which is a longtime favorite of the interpreter to say to Him. Unbelievable! After saying the prayer and waiting on the Lord's response this was seen. A very large hospital bed with a child resting with several tubes attached came as a shock, only because of the way the Lord responded immediately with the vision, which is more than just pictorial, there is a tender child being cared for by hospital personnel, and with Jesus standing close-by to comfort. Jesus just takes you into a new frame of mind. "I'm bedside with the kids still," He says. Praise the Lord. He did say that with visible dark words appearing to explain. "I care about everyone who becomes sick. I will be by your side as well," our Godly King tells us. We couldn't write a new Bible, but these "Immediate Messages Sent from Heaven" are colossal. "Good Lord, I need to be taken up higher in heaven to see," the interpreter requested. "The light is special," God and Jesus replies as soft gold angel wings point upward, with the only divide that would be was the space between the two of them.

Many interesting levels were where red flowers appeared to be inside of assorted planter boxes. The difference between them was that each arrangement was heightened inside of the heavens. Three very pretty pink flowers with straight petals without sharp edges were formed in perfect shape. A bulging white flower with a short stem even enriched the arrangement more so.

"It would help to talk about people coming through to visit with you," the Lord just told the interpreter. Vibrant pink spaced between light glows on a level surface. Also two red flowers add beauty. The Lord is also praying really hard, told from the look on His face and with grasped hands in front of Himself, asking for the right answers to come. He knew all along what they'd be, but the Lord wants us to appreciate that He is asking God for them.

"You're a scholar in our eyes," Jesus is saying. We do perk up when we hear from Him and God, and let's not forget the most charming Virgin Mary. More flowers after that was said. Three white flowers with a yellow one between them in a simple arch. A couple more very slender white candles and orange flames of light. "To let you know we are thinking of you," Jesus says. Then someone said, "You didn't catch that." Some sort of flat dark feature appeared, almost like an outlined illustration. Many different angles of this object came into view now. It was the Bible laying flat. Funny how the Lord shifted the good book around many times.

"There are people in heaven who look like that," a neat message from the Lord. A man and woman wearing dark shades came through, instantly known as "beatniks" from our point of view, at least if we judged this person with her arm raised closely to her ear, when clicking her fingers to music, that which she must be listening to with her friend. They look really cool. The two make you wonder about what they're seeing with dark sunglasses on in heaven. Probably "out of sight" for them. We can find out how much different it is to see inside of the light wearing glasses such as those. All the interpreter needs to do is fold his hands and ask in prayer. Through the Lord and His friends the answer will arrive.

"Jesus, what do they see in the light with dark glasses on?" asked in a short prayer. "Please don't look away from them," the Lord replied. The man is wearing a white robe with a black v-neck. Just the opposite with her. A black robe with a white v-neck filled in blouse or undergarment for her. "The light is very lucid still. The Lord is by my side," she comments. But the Lord couldn't possibly be the beatnik, could He? And, if they are not beatniks, they're pretty hip. A tremendous amount of full circles of golden light shines brighter than ever seen anywhere during this lifetime. An accomplishment of the Lord. "They know how you view them," Jesus is saying. Back to the people wearing sunglasses in heaven. Vibrant pink and smooth yellow openings of light were viewed through their glasses just now.

"Take them into the aspects of heaven slowly," was a statement from the Lord. The Lord and Father God have a good point there. God has to be in agreement. Why would we ever want to rush through heaven as fast as we can? Can you see us arriving there putting on our track shoes so we could race on through the heavens to see as much as we could? Even if we were to move in slow motion we'd be in heaven from what we were feeling. The touch of the Lord with the peaceful conditions of heaven.

"Ponds are many in the light," the Lord says, as several white swans are coasting along the waters. They are there beautifully filling the scenery up with the idea that spirituality is anew. Until fully known, the Holy Spirit was believed to be skimming very fast across water in movement. Now when the Lord's magnificent maneuvering revealed a sudden upward move too, into an arch, the spirit created a large angelical presence. Golden light still glows in the background where much of heaven awaits. Four baby blue candles at different heights appear out front where white flickers of light are glowing over the eternal lit sticks.

A golden keyhole appears. Then a gold key outside of the lock. "Words come through me still. You hesitate a little for a reason," Jesus is speaking. Tiny sparkling golden lights appear even farther in the background of the blue candlesticks. The key should be spoken of. It's perceptible that the key fits into a round lock. A small one. "Unlock the wisdom in your mind it will benefit many who will try to believe in the message," the information from the Lord. You'd think, he's pulling my leg isn't he? "No, I am not," the Lord continues to speak through your interpreter with visible words appearing in the air.

"My children are a success in my eyes," Jesus happened to say right now just at the right time in life for all of us to hear from Him. His heart is pouring out unto all of us, the love from deep within inside of Him is healing. Good Lord, can't you feel His Holy Spirit touch you right at this moment? He is touching your mind, body and soul. Your pain should be leaving you right now. The Holy Spirit just touched your interpreter so much that every last ounce of pain inside seemed to be just suddenly set free. It is the wonder working power of the Lord coming over you. Some people will think they are feeling a healing as well. Feeling that others are more deserving won't due in the Lord's mind, He feels you are all in need of healing and spiritual comfort. "You are deserving too," Jesus tells us. He just said that, and what a surprise.

"Thank you very much Jesus," expressed to Him. Now only if cancer would ease up inside of the many who are living with it day in and day out. "Believe in healing," appears in simple letters spelled out inside of a holy vision inside of the Holy Spirit. A really neat banner of sorts. It came in black lettered wording. Many people on the other side have small lines of lemon yellow appearing near their mouths. It was thought to be bread in communion, maybe glowing with a special spiritual light, or from breathing, but it is a little bit of both.

"Praise the Lord for your presence," to the Lord from the interpreter today. "I like the way you think," Jesus responded. He is visibly present, while holding His hand's fingers gently against His right ear to let us know how well He listens to us. The Lord said, "I know your voice, and I know everyone's voice." Stubborn children need answers right away, which is no exception in the interpreter's case. A gold lock is keeping a white treasure chest secure.

"I would want you to unlock the mysteries of the spirit world at times," the Lord says, when displaying words in the Holy Spirit to record. A white chrysanthemum appears. "They were placed on earth for human beings to ponder over." Figure out if Jesus had said that, or if it was good clean knowledge, or just intelligibly both which was stated. White light as soft as silk, but also billowy excited the mind a little by the purity. If we could only step into that light we would really have it made for an eternity. Our bare feet would be touched with the heavenly splendor.

Loud whistling won't make your spiritual visions appear any faster than they normally would. "We are aware that you are excited by the Holy Spirit. Think of the bright light until something similar comes," Jesus shared such knowledge. A small black tepee forms itself.

It hadn't a center to it, only some soft whiteness between the black illustration coming from up high. "Your errors have already been taken into account. I can make everything right," our Lord send His voice through the spirit unto us inside of our homes.

The Lord's prayer hands are presently pressed together and pointing upward even though on an angle which is meant to be of sacredness. Jesus is telling the interpreter, "Tell them I know of their pain inside and would like to relieve it immediately." You can carry on a regular conversation with the Lord and Father God. Using as much knowledge and knowhow you can shore up, they'll listen, respond, and will help you feel much better from all heartache. A yellow tulip appeared inside a little bit larger of a vanilla color flower. Jesus nudges the light in His favor as He comes inside of the same color of light which was of the vanilla color. It makes sense, if He forms a flower in such a nature. He may as well be relishing what He has created inside of their holy light above. Brilliant gold light pours out from heaven and one gold star comes with it. The Lord's right hand has smooth gold light upon it, but where is His other hand at? Suddenly His left hand, on a side view, raises ever so slightly just far enough above the right to let it be known that they were folded all along.

Is this strange? Maybe it isn't since the message is from Jesus. A large cow and a baby calf appear so unusual like, because of where they were inside of the interpreter's home. It's a vision, don't worry. Then the Lord's words appeared, "Don't worry about drinking milk it is safe."

That huge vibrant green light has come across our path again. It's not only memorable, but very frequent as a sensation now. There are ways to see it on your own, such was advised. The green light is very visible and clear. "Because of our nature we allow it to be open to the people. That's a good thought to begin with," our Master and Lord of all light relates. They take much interest in us being active on our side. "You're viewed closely at all times," also spoken from inside the heavens.

A dark baseball bat and a huge ball appears to get the point across. Baseball games can be seen in heaven, and there was a person tilting a bag of popcorn forward to show that there are treats to eat while enjoying that very enjoyable event. They would have you believe there is entertainment of all kinds. You might find that to be very unusual eating because of having a change in your digestive track, being of all light manifestation, the Holy Spirit believes it is close enough to know of too. "You need to be a little more relaxed," the Holy Spirit talks about.

The above is all true, and it's quite a change from one minute to the next that a human could go from a very relaxed feeling inside to being more intense in areas of the body. The Holy Spirit is right about us needing continual comfort. Words keep coming through the light. Let's see if this was to be interpreted. "We will abide you with pleasantness on our side. Believe me sons and daughters," Jesus said, and it was from Him, since He leaned forward to reveal who said everything. "Oh, you can have love in your life, you're just a little stubborn," Jesus adds to the mix. Maybe the interpreter isn't the only one who needed to hear that today. When Jesus speaks we need to let Him be. He is saying, "You are fortunate enough to have a daughter who loves you. If you are alone be open to conversation more often," Jesus helps us with realization.

Jesus came in an oval gold light, and in a split-second He appeared a few feet away, not detracting any of the light from sudden movement, non whatsoever. At first it was thought to be a circular light which surrounded His face, but a second look confirmed He was definitely within an oval bright light from heaven. He sharpened the vision for better viewing pleasure. Jesus is saying, "If you whisper my name I will show you." Funny how that works. The interpreter knows Jesus will reveal Himself, like He just did, but it was another open opportunity to see what would happen from His immediate instructions for others seeing Him come through in golden light. After whispering His name, for the interpreter, He appeared in all white light of Himself. His crown was even white which is alright, because in His kingdom we know it is pure gold and quite pointy still. He just changes His appearance. He also was facing two directions, actually the bust of Himself. So either God is His twin, or He is faster than lightening and can hold anyone's attention as long as He wants. But He would like everyone listening to whisper His name today. Expect Him to show you how He can be extra special to you.

There's backing up movement going on. Spiritual activity goes into other directions besides forward, sideways, or up and downward. The Lord thinks it is true. God seems to be working with arched figures in yellow and in white. Inside the scenery of heaven, there we have it proven. Small yellow candles are raging in bright candlelight upon a small white cake. Very golden and pretty. The golden burn from all the candles came together making one flame which is thick and begins to weave all around at the base of the cake, until it finally flows upward and upon the entire cake. "We know you need time to understand," they comfort us with that thought, likely coming from the Lord, since the message and cake came from inside of the holiest Holy Spirit known to us. Similar to twinkling silver stars, they've decorated the trim to our Lord's cake.

Time to hear from God again. Likely a fabricated story? No, God can communicate through His people in many different ways, all depending on the special gift received, and or from the teachings He has given us through His golden words inside of the Bible. He will speak now. If you find it hard to believe in that He will begin messaging you, don't be foolish and shun Him. "Ok God, we are ready," said in prayer. Soft blueness comes out from hiding, there inside of the heavens it remains, but it did spread into our earthly level.

"Don't think of me as selfish. I'm here as much as the Lord is," God most certainly did say using visible wording to render. A sliver of baby blue light comes back in the form of the number one. "In comparison to what you saw. They will think you are accurate," said to us. A very tight fist in blue and a sparkle of gold is a message from God about fighting. "You should settle your differences peacefully instead," God is trying to tell us. He indisputably did say that.

At the same time the interpreter wondered if the Holy Spirit might be a little bit of the same when a soft pink candle disappeared. And with half a thought or even somewhat more of one forming, it was pondered how anything so beautiful in the spirit could ever fade away.

God was testing one's faith in Him as well. How could we ever tire of hearing what He says out loud, or even for what He and His Son and Mary show us at the onset of our journey home? "Not a bad thought," the Holy Spirit sent through the communiqué. Small and large ivory angel wings are here now. Someone inside of the wings is giggling, always a favorite sign from the holy land. So cute and acceptable. Unless the angel just "burped" and was holding a hand up to her mouth. By the way she looks it is mostly her chuckling with laughter. "It's a cute story you have," her words appeared as to what she wanted to convey to the interpreter and for everyone else as well. "Thank you," from the interpreter. A glowing glow comes from her lantern in her right hand, but the widely spread out ruffled wings is what really is eye-catching. The lantern's light instantly started glowing with light. For some reason the light is softer. Three balls of golden light shine in front of the angelic woman with long curls of golden hair to her shoulders. She was now fully covered from head to toe, and boy oh boy does she every glitter. The Bible is all gold, extended out for reading. She makes sure it became known that she enjoys knowing about the Lord. A large "V" appears. Words read: Victory is Ours.

Wouldn't we like to know if our government is hiding something from us? Let's see if we can get the scoop on them. "I wonder if there's anything we should know about, Lord?" the interpreter asks in a short prayer to be heard and answered if possible. "Your government is forthright mainly. They have problems in their inner circle mostly," a message from above. A white light shines over the White House. "You have a powerful nation. All nations are just as equal," the Lord sent by way of an instant message.

A streak of golden light and a glittering silver crown happened to come into sight. "Mary knows you admire Her. Bring Her into the conversation if you like," Jesus says, but He instructed to pray first as His hands were seen in three positions. That was done to get our attention first. "Mary, please come to us through the light," from an interpreter eager to learn. Unusual movement happed. Beautiful silver, white and a only a small blue color of light appears twice. But it was spectacular to see, nothing else could compare. It is sensed that

Mary is ready to appear, but perhaps She is waiting for you to see her first. "My time with you will be spent wisely. You are beginning to understand me," visible words shown as such. She looks like Jesus more, with both coming through Her facial image. "I am one is why you thought what was believed. Love everyone for me," Mary said, and you can tell of Her Motherly instinct. "Please be kind instead of rude." She knows that the interpreter has been somewhat rude in the past. Hopefully Her wisdom will prevail, only to be applied more often. When wondering about who Mary is with on the other side, She said, "I am with everyone."

A woman in golden white light is overwhelmed. An example of how she felt about God, how He created Himself. Overall His uniqueness. Her mouth is open and she is surprised to know the truth. And this time the interpreter only had to think about how God was born before an answer was given. Their example came of how people react when they first discover how He did it. They respond to us through our silent meditations. "You will think it is very interesting how God planned your life," the Lord said, and He even pointed to the very first word that appeared in the formation of black lettering.

"Our side is jubilant in spirit. I'm on your side too," Jesus is saying. He did glance at the interpreter again. What's unique is this, a new day and the Lord is still here with you and me. A thick curl of white light formed twice with a small ivory angel decorating them with a gold cross, and a piece with various golden bells that glitter. "Try to understand the Lord is helping people every day," coming from the other side in words, but it is anyone's guess who said that. We will not pressure the Lord for the answer, we will just believe it arrived by the grace of God.

We can receive a message from Elvis if you're at all interested. They say, "They will think he's crazy, but it's possible." Now who'd you think they were talking about being a little nuts, the interpreter or our famous person within the spiritual contact? We don't need to hold a seance for Elvis to appear in the light. "Can we contact Elvis today, Lord?" asked in the Holy Spirit from an individual prayer. "I played for the masses and enjoyed every day when I was there," Elvis reveals. Are you jealous? Of the interpreter being able to communicate with Elvis! He is holding onto a guitar and looking at the front of it very close. "Thank you for relating a message for me," he said, and there is really no need to explain him having a way with demonstrating words from his side, it's still his voice pattern within them too. What's he wearing? "I have a religious side that I cherish too," he casually mentioned. A large gold star appears, much bigger than most seen from heaven in awhile. Elvis is wearing a white robe with a white carnation over his heart. The gold cross in the middle of his chest helps him grow inside. He says, "I pondered drugs often and felt I was doing the wrong thing." It is hard to believe he is here in the white light appearing above, behind, and around his shoulders. "My guitar was everything to me tell them," he says. He's close to returning to heaven now. "We feel his journey to earth was helpful," the Holy Spirit announces. "I joined a choir here," he wanted known. That message came quickly. The very white light inside of the Holy Spirit has covered Elvis. They say, "Elvis is a choir member now." And you wonder what the difference would be from hearing that over again? Elvis said it the first time, and the Lord mentioned it to be heard for reassurance.

Your yearning for heaven to open up is stronger than of many if you've come this far without complaining. Visualize feet walking around below, where your feet rest view the movement. Look for a big toe first of all. The toes and feet of the Lord shall follow. You should see brown strapped sandals upon His feet, more to His liking. Bands of golden light should extend across the floor, if not soothing white and blue light. You will be wise enough to be able to see the Lord's feet in a walking position, one foot in step ahead of the other. Perhaps they will be still. He is raising His right foot. Now He is facing forward, according to the direction He has taken and the great visibility of our Lord's feet. The bottom edge of His white robe is shaped like an angel's wing. "I would be pleased if they see me," Jesus explains. He disclosed that forty percent of the people looking for them will see His feet and robe during this period. That was due to a vision of the number and the percentage symbol. Snow white lines across the floor were looked at now, and let's see what we have here. The Lord's right foot is slanted down, which meant He was taking a step. There were stairs in the light. Those stairs are close at hand. "I will be ready when you arrive," Jesus said, when using golden words which were sharp enough to see.

Loose floorboards are buckling. "We will walk beside you when it's rough. There are examples to help you along the way," the Holy Spirit wanted said. Many expanding white bells clearly spread out everywhere is a welcoming sign. Words read: Welcome to heaven. They're not fussy about the way they spell. Two children with yellow and soft blue haloes hold their heavenly white candle in front of themselves. "You know us already. Expect to be taken many fun places," they are saying. If you don't believe that, that's okay for now. A well-strung guitar appears, but it isn't the one Elvis had. White light glows between every string. A player of that guitar wears a red flower that's neatly tucked into her very full head of brown hair. That is hair very well kept and bushy. "I love you because of the Lord," she said while wonderful white light soothes her face. Maybe you can figure out how she did what she did just now. She is lying flat on her back playing the guitar as she is very much in her own comfort zone. She's right handed.

She is standing again. Her arms really stretch out far quickly, one at a time, you'd think she was stretching taffy. "That's interesting," she responds to the reference made. The Holy Spirit moves quickly with superior performance. Everything thus far has been greatly appreciated. "Thank you from Jesus," was said. And He is very welcome, and likely the Lord is examining this transcription closely still. Just daydream for awhile capturing the entire living space which you are able to see within the scope of your home. When the mind is at ease you will drift off into heaven faster. We have a doctor inside of the mild orange light reaching into his black bag for a stethoscope.

Be patient and still. You do need to know what the numbers mean in the future," he spoke of by magically making himself and words appear. That's what people meant by a doctor making a house call. He came from heaven. But leaving one's body unexpectedly, how do we know that he wasn't just visiting in heaven, while one's mind has traveled to see him, which was the other way around?

"Recent with someone," was the message from our friends in heaven, as there were special white flowers covering the entire top of a long casket. "People spend their entire life grieving over loved ones. It was a woman who passed recently," the thoughts are conveyed kindly from the Holy Spirit. She was loved by everyone who is there in heaven. "Rejoice because your soul is free," is a new message, and we shall try to remember that God and the Lord have prepared us already. The beaming soft orange light in heaven comes from a special tunnel and all of the white flowers upon the casket are of newness now. They have become orange flowers that are so soft.

The Holy Spirit does so many wonderful things, right now they are making the interpreter curl his toes back, the visibility is so stunning that words merely won't give all of the justice that they deserve. But we will try. A blue ray now shoots across the room, while a lighter shade followed that. "I will make it happen," says the Lord. He already did, and what He really meant by His very own words appearing in the light was that the whole remaining story He has to tell will be created from His very own way of conveying everything in spirit. In all likelihood, though, He'll be joined by His Mother Mary and Father God.

"Turn to the Lord for comfort," Jesus said, while that message came across easily from observing in the heavens again. There's a pitchfork standing tall. Then a square bale of hay appears. "It's helpful for the spirit to tell you," heard from above now. Green beans, corn and a peeled potato is illustrated. Everything sounds so familiar for those of us who understand farming. "You should know why I show you these things," the Lord announces. We do know why the Lord and Almighty God have given us farmland to grow such foods. So we can survive, even if it means growing our own fruits and vegetables in our backyards, we have their blessing from above. "Care about your neighbors," talked about through the spirit.

They think the interpreter has an idea what to say, but nothing happens until the Grand Masters ruling heaven and earth forward the information. "I think I need to be lifted higher into the Holy Spirit, Lord," asked for in prayer, "You asked for it," the Holy Spirit responded. And it doesn't matter how their English happened to sound, it's the wonderful genius of a genius mind at work with us. The Dutch are coming back through the light. Such beautiful head wear for these women. They are big in heaven, no doubt. "You need to translate in English. The Netherlands is where I originated from," a woman is explaining. She is really overwhelmed, with hands pressing firmly against her face, her fingers curling backward is telling she is expressive. Heaven and the people there will be more exciting than where we are.

"Spain is a special country too. Iraq is a troubled country," the Holy Spirit interjected. It seems odd that we would jump over to these countries when we were having so much fun with the lady with the very lively personality. "I'm still here but you needed to know something else," she comes back to say to us. Now someone is saying, "Disasters do continue to occur." "The Dutch feel there is an important message to be said," a friend of our friendly woman was filling us in on. Known she was a friend was that of her lovely well-noted white cap in comparison from the first woman's very tan bonnet upon her head. "You make us smile too," the women from Dutch living in heaven are saying. Secretly the interpreter thought about how they were able to bring such great happiness from a place so far away inside of the light. "Farewell for now," spoken.

A spirit begins lifting upward, but how Godly is the movement? Several glowing circular balls of light extended flat made the letter "A". No lines, just creative form of the letter. Tint ivory angels with them moving their wings up have a look of real concern as they have facial expressions too. They have a voice and they are wondering if the people of the world have gone a little crazy. That word "crazy" appeared with earlier wording. Funny how such little angels have the ability to lead. "I will permit you to say that," the Lord helped with launching us into the spirit world more, as He spoke up again.

A combination of silvery white lines make a holy cross now. It is quite a distance away and still very visible with white light up inside of the kingdom of God sandwiched in between a much smaller golden cross. When we feel something is right it is helpful to believe in our gut, intuitively, that is the will of God in our lives. The Lord says, "I have instilled the intuitive side in everyone. Examine your feelings thoroughly before you act." It was hard saying why this came up, maybe it was just the curious side of how we will look in heaven.

The Holy Spirit moved in such an upward wiggly way that they seemed to be showing that there was a very comfortable chair that we would be able to rest upon when with them. It was though the vision was also of the human spine which one could see without the fleshy part attached. It gets better. "You will have many body parts including the torso," the Holy Spirit sent in a message. Uncommon but true. We would automatically believe that everything inside is of eternal light, which it will always be of, as our own characteristics are.

The Lord is sitting at a side view of Him in soothing white light now. He showed the global earth nearby, telling us He is here to help non-stop. His right hand was of golden light. He brought his hand across His mid section to touch the stomach, and intestine area. "Make them believe what I showed you was true," He says. Jesus wants us to think and believe that the glowing gold light is to help with matters of physical healing. Although the interpreter was starting to think that it should be drawn in just from the hand to the mid section, the Lord interjects by appearing larger than life with a Fathering golden light behind His head that spreads within Him beautifully. Good Lord, that He is. "Believe a healing is coming," dear Jesus says, and boy oh boy does the Holy Spirit feel warm right now. Too much of a good thing indeed. The Interpreter hopes you are feeling the touch of the Holy Spirit too. "Thank you Jesus. Thank you God," from the interpreter to both whom are present and distributing gifts of warmth and love inside of the Holy Spirit. That was truthfully unexpected. "Expect more healing to come in the near future," Jesus explains. But Jesus wanted to remind us of drawn in eternal light of color to "if we must" imagine to be entering through the back to our hands, inside, and on top of our flesh to press gently upon our affliction. Although most of the Lord's light that travels within.

Faraway in the distance there is a golden castle, and the domain has a gigantic gold crown right above it. Jesus brings Himself in through the spirit. Parts of Him appear, but we know He is whole still. He's sparkling in all gold, to where it thickens upon His chest, the left sleeve and elbow which were seen. He says, "Tell them time is of the essence." More or less of time being of substance. Jesus is showing the state of Florida again. He says, "You better look at it as something new." The year of 2015 in numerals are in sight. And the words, "gusty winds." Likely for Spring and summer so be prepared. "They'll be safe if they throw caution to the wind," He added. It was a good thing.

A wise man with a spread beard comes to us inside of vanilla white light, holding a large cup. He said, "Drink and be merry." His cup is pouring very soft golden drink back into a fairly large pitcher which rests upon a small pearly white stand. "Giving back helps. There are many favorite drinks absorbed," he attests to of in the spirit. We shall have a pleasant stay.

Multi colors sparkle a little inside of a triangle. Gold and black come together in a meaningful vision of eternal colors. People have been rescued by the Lord at sea recently. Even though a message was given in private from the Lord, it is most obliging of Him to bring that up. "It's better that you accept what has happened," His message was. They all came to the Lord. "It's magic how they enter the kingdom," our Lord says. Your interpreter was wondering about that, how the people of aboard down jetliners would penetrate through the outer shell of the plane to go up to heaven. "An example will be made for you," Jesus is saying. A man can be seen boosting himself up out from the top of a plane, but first it seemed he was doing a pushup. Here we go. "I was aboard," the man is saying, as he too can send telepathic messages using visible words. "He doesn't think he knows what to say," the man sent in a message to the Lord, who in return sent this back to the interpreter in a message. Kind of funny. Tell them, "All aboard arrived safely." What can we as an understanding crowd of people do but nod our heads back to him. We certainly do appreciate and approve of his message. How do you like that? People involved with serious accidents, not only do they have assistance from God and the

Lord and from their angels lifting them up to their new home, but there is an option of beginning to help yourself to go on now.

Two red roses with a yellow flower in the center of them was a gift in the Holy Spirit, brought down to below where we live, to be seen and remembered that the crew and attendants aboard are very special people who think about everyone else on earth who were thinking of them. They even said, "From the people aboard." There is no way on God's green earth that the interpreter would make that up with the eyes of God upon him. Those spiritual people feel that they are very relieved, and you would probably enjoy hearing a little bit about someone, inside of the Holy Spirit, closely related to them a man salutes while standing at attention.

"The word is of good spirit," an Indian of the manly type says while appearing with the Bible in his hands. His roots were important to him, as a person living he had many children. "It was a little unusual seeing them growing older than myself. White men were a thorn in our side, you might say," he mentions. But still the Lord believes that we are all as of one people in the unity of Christ. We must have woke up several tribes in the heavens. Many full headdresses in vibrant colors have come alive. Many smaller children are touching, wearing one black feather a piece. The Indian chiefs were easily seen as well as the youngsters, but when receiving messages from the first Indian with the larger family, he took some doing in seeing who he was, and for what reason he was here to begin with. He finally came in clearer when squinting some. The Indian boy who poked his head in like someone diving forward, that was more unbelievable than the rest, he just took control over all invisibility. Just soft feathers for the other children were seen, but activity beneath them suggested people were moving beneath the individual feather they were wearing upon their head.

Even though the interpreter was unable to figure out exactly what he saw just now, the other side of life can still place one's mind in a soothing tranquil state of being. You know when you are thinking so deeply that everything seems almost pitch dark. Kind of hard to explain unless you've been there before. God and the Lord were demonstrating a beam of orange light connected by a swirling soft, black tether, which met together with a golden line of light. Not numb chucks if you know what fighting sticks are. The tether had black strands. "It was a whip of sorts," the Holy Spirit is saying, confirming what your interpreter was thinking all along. It should be quite interesting what the Lord has to add on about what He just said. "By my stripes you are healed," was a visible worded message given from Him right now.

We have a little giggle box in the spirit again. While pondering the beauty in the white lily flower that came first, it seemed peculiar one narrow golden leaf would be sticking up from behind. And then there were two golden shapes in back of the flower. The tiniest face of an angelical girl popped up too, right between her God given golden wings of magnificence. She revealed that her halo is a golden circle above her head, and there was a thin white line extending from her back to the very bottom for support. It holds up nicely. What a divine sight, and it makes for really good artwork if you were an artist and would be willing to paint a picture of her and the lovely flower. She just said, "Oops!" That word was spelled out near her. She's still giggling. "We make you wonder about us," she was saying.

A soft ball of white light with a miniature characteristic of the same attached to it has a black stem. A little loss for words until the spirit moves the interpreter again. "You should think of it like that," the Lord sent through, when relating to more signs and wonder. While thinking the visual to be of an enchanted wonder, that's what it was. Wouldn't you like to grab hold of that black colored stick and twirl the two balls of white light around in circles? Maybe in various other directions too, to see what the smaller ball attached within that dimension of the light would do while circling. Now if someone could try and invent some sort of fascinating toy or grownup game from this. Apparently the Lord is showing us that there is a first step with everything planned. One thing for sure is that the white light is getting closer and closer when thinking about the two balls of white light. A silver lining of light is glorifying the larger ball. But let it be fully realized that we are experiencing an out of body situation, not an illusion.

The Lord says, "Speak your mind, and that was while believing He was sending a pink vibration down. "You can tell them what you saw," Jesus is confident in saying. As the Holy Spirit rises into the heavens the Lord is innocently watching His flock. The tenderness in His eyes, the soft expression of His face, and the easiness in Him tells us the Lord is very peaceful. A look on Him as if He were saying, "Where are you going, I love you, and please don't leave me." He didn't need to display words inside of His divine Holy Spirit, He's here before us, and if you happen to gaze upward for a moment, He will appear posthaste.

While bowing forward, the golden crown shined brightly sending forth an immediate ray of light down to earth, to where it suddenly appeared that only an opening of white eternal light was descended inside of the spiritual realm which reaches out to us. You'd love to walk into that light. Why the change? For the reason of knowing the Lord is much more appreciable than ever. That brilliant crown of golden light is aglow though, now more than ever, where He remains in ultimate rulership upon the throne of attraction. "I am willing to acknowledge your wishes," the Lord is expressing using a darker formation of bold print words in English. No better time than the present to pour out your heart to the Lord, after all, He is present during the transcription.

A really young lady appearing near twenty years of age, softly from such holy intervention, spreads out two sets of very small ivory wings. First from above her shoulders and then pointed ruffled wings from behind them. But the interpreter may have to take back that the wings were very small, unless it was her just changing the second set behind her into a bigger size all at once. So the interpreter was right. Any ways, before she went through changes the smaller set of wings had developed into more of a larger opening to where they seemed like thick flower petals blooming in a very rich ivory color. Then an enlargement was more evident, not to confuse one with the other. A thin, drooping, brightly lit white and ivory mixed halo appeared above her.

A funny girl. She is shifting a white carnation back and forth. The same girl as aforementioned. "I wish you would believe in miracles," she tells us. With all of the immediate attention we are receiving we are bound to have one fall into our laps anytime now. Again, her angelical wings are going through changes. Her four wings stretch out forming into a large petaled ivory flower, but she doesn't appear, just the flower's emergence.

"God, do you feel old?" the interpreter asks in prayer. "Not in the least," was His answer with magical words appearing before the interpreter's eyes. Magnificent soft blue bursted from the heavens, surrounding someone who resembles the Lord. And He's resting on a throne made from ivory. He looks a little Chinese, but then again with the look embedded inside His eyes, our visitor is more Japanese with a beard and mustache which is chestnut. "Expect me to look unusual," He is saying. Well, He is really more brown and black now. That's the truth, His face changed, one side black, and the other full cheek area is brown. From one color He went to the two tone stage. Two ivory rings are attached in His nostrils with His skin turning completely pale. The first thought was "albino." "Expect something to be said behind the scenes," He mentions, and it will be pertaining to what is being said right here.

Thick layers of black satin unravel. "There will be a gift made to your taste," our friendly Holy Spirit Master in the light has so lovingly announced on this very special day of life. Someone's arms are folded in while trying on an outfit of clothing that bears a striking resemblance to that black satin, but there are many silver stars on this attire. Two huge feet are coming. Sounds offbeat but we will find who it is. He is laughing while in white and toned down orange light from the other side. Now the feet are side by side and the spiritual guide is wearing dark sandals. Sounds like Jesus is here with us. Perhaps that's white cloth draped over His feet now. Right in view prayer hands rest upon the level where His feet are, which is the foundation of heaven. Very manly is He. The noticed veins in His feet are beneath the top layer of His feet, not uncommon for the Lord or for God to be very much like the rest of us. The spirits in heaven have slight advantages of not carrying around all of the extra physical weight since they have the amazing ability within to be free in the light world. That includes their superficiality. We won't exactly be light as a feather all of the time, but pretty close to that. We shall never feel trapped inside.

Here goes everything. Smooth flowing silver rivers come from the heavenly light itself, where many are enjoying the sounds of the river's flow with life exalting around everyone. Oversized tan, white and even softer colored gold boats have people in them upon these waters which carry them on an adventure in heaven. Not the only way to get around by no means. "We know you are enthused about the spirit world," a younger man says as he curls his lip and tilts his head back slightly, during the conversation of visible wording coming from him through soft white light. He can see us as they travel through the splashing water. Bright golden light opens the heavens even wider. One thing for sure there are huge oars being used on the waters as well. Any closer and they would have clobbered the interpreter.

Little four leaf clovers are popping up from several clusters. The sun is now covering them with so much light that they are more orange looking, which is quite wondrous. "Expect the unusual to happen," says the Lord. He has spoken like that before, so we really do know that it is a message coming from our King and Godly Lord. White lilies blend in with the magical four leaf clovers. They are so delicate in the light. Could it be God still experimenting with His flowers, transforming, and coloring them more to His own delight? "To prepare you for the following message," comes from either the Lord or from God, Himself, sent through while showing many smaller facets. There are so many features to heaven, when they change so often, one's mind has to decide how to decipher. It feels like someone is walking with a lively spring in their step, just moseying on by and singing. If you were deaf and saw the flowing spirit exhibiting the natural flow of zeal in the light, you'd already suspect that someone was singing.

Helped with trainers small children are riding upon the backs of Shetland ponies. They can be seen in heaven inside that very tranquil state of life. The Lord just sends you to heaven when He so desires that you see who He does, and who He believes that should be acknowledged. Funny how the little ones are leaning forward, and they don't even look more than seven and eight years old. Again, why would they have to be taken away at such a young age? God only knows, but believe in your heart that these children, and if you have one or two of your own who've left earlier on to be with Jesus, all of the lovable children in heaven are very cheerful.

Can this be true, more supernatural insight again? The Holy Spirit is very much in with the timing of saxophone music being heard. The sound comes from a personal preference, but as it plays on with a very upbeat temple the Lord's spirit keeps in step with every other instrument involved with the melody. "We enjoy the way it sounds," Jesus says, but it is uncertain if everyone will believe in Him. More is coming again. "We know that it is an unusual step in the light," He also added. If we could have the chance to dance and be merry such as He is, only a mere fraction of how He feels in the Holy Spirit would be enough to send us sailing away in our minds. For an example, the Lord has a visitor tilting forward a pair of shiny black dance slippers. There is a side strap. Felt that a person is slipping them on would be correct, because as of now there's a beautiful lady about forty years old balancing herself on her tiptoes.

She is a happy person relaxing in soothing golden white light with the look of poise. Her white dress is soft with golden flowers. The dress is not long, and her legs show from the knee down. The dress also seems crystal like. "Ballerinas are a common sight in heaven. The little ladies are very cute when they dance," she speaks kindly of them. She holds a flower bouquet in her right hand down by her side and she leans. As she swirls around the bouquet is visibly being raised and lowered in the different quadrants of space. She has either her golden straight hair tied into a small bow upon the top of her head, or she is wearing one that is matching the features.

Come again? A dainty off white angel no bigger than a hummingbird is present. The angel is accommodating with magic. First the tips of the wings start sparkling in gold. Then the little bitty baby angel bows. And the wings suddenly turned all white, while the angel seems to be thanking us. "They are adorable," comes from a higher voice in the hereafter. The Holy Spirit made a huge black anvil disappear. The other side says, showing words, "Loose the weight." It can also mean to rid ourselves of unnecessary anguish too, because your interpreter surely doesn't have too much physical weight. And then again, they must be speaking to everyone. Jesus was right when He said that our messages would be unusual.

"Obstacles will be removed if you yield. You know the truth," the Lord speaks to all. A man standing in a crowd of fighters feels there should be peace instead. "I'm listening to what was brought to me in prayer," the Lord says, as the man down below has been praying in disbelief. The troubled man is hindered by trouble on foreign territory. The name of the country Iraq appeared, when spelled out. "Too much bloodshed in the past," the Lord said, which was seen through the message. And we complain about the little things, which we should let go of. "I really think fighting is wrong," Jesus wanted to mention. The Lord knows best.

"My followers visit you," also a spiritual message now. While trying to figure out who they were, the Lord interrupted to set the record straight. He was just in doing so. The first saintly fellow had very white hair, a mustache and a super long beard that blew in the wind. He has one of thickest books in history sitting near his feet. He tapped the cover and instantly he was at the very first page. He does wish people happiness, this much is true. In the corner of his left eye a golden sparkle lit up, and there he was with brown eyes when all was said and done. So darn clear. He walks with the Shepherd's cane, but in a smaller version of what the Lord gently holds to His side. Hopefully the interpreter hasn't said anything wrong to upset the supernatural visitor. His Shepherd's cane just grew two feet and then a couple more in height. There's a spirit more instep. A small gold and white cross appear together.

He says, "Tell them I want to be a friend to them." "Yes you are nice," the interpreter tells him. Reference to one of the friendly spirits who was just here. You know Jesus will use your name when He tells you how much He loves you. The Lord says, "Tell them to visualize their name in bold letters." Take out a minute of your day to look for that vision of your name to come through. You know how it looks in bold black print, now expect the Lord to show you how He communicates in the spirit with wording. Once you have asked the Lord to start showing you word messages starting with your first name, tell Him to add words with your name in the message. God will do the same for you. You might want to look at lower case as well. Hanging your head down to look around slowly would help a great deal. Don't be afraid of the spirit world, they're very kind and understanding.

Now back to the second visitor minutes ago. Even though some time has passed on our side, the visitor would like to share his feelings. He's sitting in prayer at a table. The white light upon him is gentle. "The transcript you read is excellent. Trust the message," an older man with short blonde hair relates as the Lord stands behind him in guidance thereof. It is nice to know that when you relay messages from heaven that they are pretty much up to snuff. Tall white rays of light which are plentiful and very soft pop up more like a rounded fence at the top and bottom. A vibrant pink shade of light is in the far background. The same area where the Lord and His friends came from. No we are not blocked off from the other side of life. Beautiful gold angels with enriched wings that spread out between the many white lights are incredible.

Now we know there are cute little baskets women carry flowers and sometimes small kittens and pawing pups around in up inside of heaven, but there is a proud young lady with one of the biggest yet seen. She's peeking in over the top edge. Let's see what we have here. All depends on her, not the interpreter. She starts things out by saying, "I come as a peacemaker." Black and white, and brown and whiter puppies with dark patches all over their furry bodies are held onto. The adorable pup who is brown, black, and a little butterscotch mixed together has both paws gently reaching over the top edge of the basket now. The pup's tongue is the cutest and slightly pink. The young lady is much younger than thought to be. She may bring a tear as she sends this important message, "Mom, I miss you." The best message heard all day. Her dress is very dark, almost charcoal and black, all in good taste. You wouldn't see a dress made on our side that pretty. We have pretty dresses, but that one is more praiseworthy. Someone else in the basket. She said, "It's a white cat it belonged to me when I was alive." What a fur ball. The yellow and white tulips surround the girl. Now she reveals her rolling curls of shoulder length hair. How could we ever believe this? We should because if we don't we'd be much worse off than we ever were. The name "John" and a large music note appeared. It was said by the Holy Spirit, "He is at a much better place." There are many people who live in the glorious heaven above us named John, people who've studied and played, sung and danced to many lively tunes. Including famous people too.

"Your family believes you will be happier when you arrive," Jesus comes back to us again with this message. Perhaps Jesus detected a little sadness in our eyes. We don't always show it but we miss our family dearly. Never feel guilty if you weren't able to do enough for them, they are watching over you and realize whatever amount of sadness you have felt about them is because of that gigantic heart filled with love for them. So when Jesus repeats Himself, feel you have received a double blessing from Him. He's trying His best to make you believe in this transliteration. "They feel it might be too much to handle," the Lord communicated now. Heaven as being hard to accept because it is so wonderful, relaxing a place as can be filled with happy children and grownup mom's and dad's cheerful voices? Everyone else too. We will feel that we need to know everything is real and well balanced, that's where we must increase our faith we have in God.

The Lord's gold crown tips forward as He has so much faith in all, that He does that. Can you believe He tipped His royal crown to you? He did and for that matter, even though the Lord's crown was only seen moments ago, believe He is still in the foreground.

Jesus says, "Carry on with your daily routine," while great motion suggests His hands are moving upward, leaving the impression He made a huge scoop too. The Lord feels people dislike the repetition of some of His messages. Maybe true, but the interpreter doesn't mind seeing some of the same vibrations of light. Such a big change though, when in the afterlife.

"Im sorry it turned out that way," one famous comedian by the name of Buster Keaton is saying in the spirit world. Looking very black and white in the spirit, he was identical to how he appeared in silent films which he directed. What Buster felt was going wrong was the interpreter not willing to move forward with His messages. It was a little selfish. But he came back through the very mystifying white holy light for a second time which helped move things along. And he was bowing down. "I felt it was necessary to appear," Buster says. What an honor to hear that, especially when feeling ordinary. "My movie career made me feel good inside. I laughed hard at times," He is telling us. Suddenly Buster has been celebrated with a golden light upon him and the Lord's sitting next to him. One can see the Lord's white robe and Buster tipping his black derby, if you look up. Yes his derby turned black above all the gold light. "I have one more thing to say. Let your heart be filled with love today," our good comedian and actor tells us. Not everyone knew who he was, but around the world there were scores of people who did.

The softest white angel is penetrating through the air. Wings are up and very transparent. "It's a soft feel here. I'm an angel too," a girl mentions. She too is within the white light. A small golden arch brightens. Many small baskets of daises are being delivered for you to appreciate. "Often you will feel blessed with flowers," she says.

You will be enlightened to know that God and the Lord haven't far to search for the answers to your questions. "Your desires will be honored," Jesus says, as He has His hands nearly fully cupped together. The reason He hasn't completely draw them together all the way is because of the bursting golden light and star inside of His hands. They seem to be plentiful, whereas the blessings department is gradually coming instead of too much at once. Their blessings are very bounteous, but we need time to appreciate them. How about the miracles? "They will come if you are obedient," Jesus replies to the interpreter's inner most thoughts.

"You will often think you are busy with social events here," the Lord says. There is control of the setting on our part as well. Do we ring doorbells in heaven when we are expected over as company? "Good question! At times to be courteous," the Lord responded during the prayer. Remember they do measure distance similar to the way we do in regards to our well being. You will have to know what distance to travel during heaven's daily routine. Time will be discussed at times which is unusual, but thought to be useful.

A small gold ladder and a white teddy bear with brown eyes tilt out from inside a large white and black box wrapped with darker ribbon. How the Lord managed to get them to pop up from the box with the wrapping still on is a marvel in itself. Jesus said, "You liked surprises as a kid." All of the kiddie talk and images brings back the spirit of Christmas. And a small baseball and rag doll appears. The Lord is definitely bowing way down in a very soothing golden light, and our Father God is doing the polite thing, following Christ's lead. The Fatherly image of God here in the Holy Spirit smiles, favoring His Son in appearance, but He's covered in more white light with a more of a very large beard and mustache. While God's fully covered with light, the Virgin Mary joins in and you can't help admiring Her silver crown is filled with glistening diamonds, red rubies, green emeralds and some very beautiful gold. Mary's crown has beauty that which comes from Her expected changes She made for Her head wear. She adjusts Her crown ever so gently, giving one thoughts of a very pleasant woman smiling happily.